*f*P

MARY BLUME

A FRENCH AFFAIR

The Paris Beat
1965–1998

Drawings by Ronald Searle

THE FREE PRESS

THE FREE PRESS
A Division of Simon & Schuster Inc.
1230 Avenue of the Americas
New York, NY 10020

Designed by Pei Loi Koay

Manufactured in the United States of America

10   9   8   7   6   5   4   3   2   1

Library of Congress Cataloging-in-Publication Data

Blume, Mary.
     A French affair: the Paris beat, 1965–1998 / Mary Blume.
         p.   cm.
     1. Blume, Mary—Homes and haunts—France—Paris.   2. National
characteristics, French—Humor.   3. Americans—France—Paris
—Attitudes.   4. Women journalists—France—Paris—Attitudes.
     5. Paris (France)—Social life and customs—20th century—Humor.
     I. Title.
944' .36—dc21   99-17142
                                                                          CIP

All the articles in this collection first appeared in the *International Herald
Tribune*.

ISBN: 0-684-86301-4

CONTENTS

WORDS AND IMAGES

CONTENTS

PREFACE

THERE ARE SO MANY RULES in France and no way to fathom or remember them. My first summer in Paris I made a tuna salad sandwich for a French friend. "One does not put fish between bread," the friend pronounced. I still don't really understand this rule, or even know if it is true, but I have never since put fish between slices of bread.

In France, it is understood that one must try to obey the rules and that one will fail, and then comes the relieving moment when it doesn't matter: the French have problems with them too, and it is one reason they are so uncomfortable with each other. Rules of grammar, rules of fish, rules of conduct, coded phrases all act to separate people but the fact that these rules exist brings comfort and even unity: it makes them French and thus unique. "Diverse in its unity, complex in its diversity, the French soul is made from contrasts which, melted together, compose a whole of rare originality," a forgotten academician wrote in *L'Ame Française* in 1936. The French are different from everyone else, which is their pride; they are also different from one another, which is their undoing.

I of course knew none of this when I drifted into the old *Herald Tribune* office off the Champs Elysées, beamish and eager and never having written, my only qualification as a journalist being the terrible typing that had made me unemployable in New York. (In those pre-computer days news copy looked like ransom notes and at *Le Figaro* reporters still wrote by hand.) The United States seemed to me bland then, and self-satisfied, the faces around me somehow (like my own) incomplete. The food had no flavor, the automobiles were too pillowy, the light too harsh. Paris was literally gray (the cleaning of every façade ordained by the novelist André Malraux in his new role as France's first minister of culture was just underway), its skies were soft and wide. Everything had a taste and, in those days of outdoor iron toilets, called *vespasiennes* and rare washing machines, a smell. There were seasons, winter dark and bone-chilling in the absence of central heating and spring like a blessing with the first asparagus and, later, the cherries. I hadn't known that in the winter the sidewalk cafés are glassed-in, in fact I knew almost nothing except that Paris was very old, and to someone young this is in itself a delight. Later, I realized that history is what France has too much of.

Probably I came in part for Paris's past, not realizing that the past is several. For many of us the Lost Generation was still alive in memory and, to a degree, in fact: I once saw Alice B. Toklas, bent with age and silkily mustached, at a gallery opening, and had I had the money I could have bought Sylvia Beach's apartment near the Odéon. There were shabby widows from both wars everywhere, mending nylons in shop windows that advertised *stoppage,* selling lottery tickets in rickety sidewalk booths, collecting a fee for letting people sit in the iron chairs in the Luxembourg Gardens or the Tuileries.

No one in the Paris of the early 1960s seemed to laugh (even a government plan to pay Parisians who smiled at tourists failed utterly). This bothered me later but at the time not at all because not laughing seemed somehow grown-up and Left Bank (I had, after all, seen pictures of glum postwar existentialists).

World War II was still too near, poisoning the atmosphere with its grief and evasions. No one talked about it except to mention the food shortages. The Parisians who had spent their youth under the Occupation seemed lethargic, ill at ease and enclosed, while the older generation who had known the interwar years were a delight—easy, debonair, generous and gay. They spoke beautiful French, whatever their class, and had a sense of pleasure all the more acute because most of them had lost family on the battlefields of World War I. What the later generation had lost in World War II was undefined—composure surely, as if the unanswered (and for a long time unposed) questions about Vichy had made them lose their footing. They had an arrogance that comes from being unsure of themselves, and each other.

They also had the president they needed, and deserved, Charles de Gaulle, a great statesman and a cynical manipulator of his countrymen. He invented the fiction that they had risen to free themselves from the Germans without help and, knowing the truth, he treated them with contempt. Normally unruly, the French were surly and cowed, more self-absorbed than ever. There was no sense of curiosity: when Buckminster Fuller, the venerable inventor of the geodesic dome and a bubbling torrent of ideas, gave an open-air lecture for Beaux Arts students of architecture almost no one came. "They're all busy drawing Doric columns," an American exchange student explained to me.

De Gaulle was a master at playing on the dual French characteristics of anarchy and tractability until boredom overcame France in 1968. (The first sign that a ramshackle students' movement might instead lead to bloodshed and nationwide alarm is now taken to be the famous *Le Monde* headline in March 1968:

Quand la France S'Ennuie, when France is bored.) And de Gaulle's France was indeed boring and self-serving. The intellectuals, riven by the Occupation and the Cold War, abandoned their public role, except for de Gaulle's tamed mythomaniac, Malraux, and retreated to private experiments in literary technique and to academe. The arts had been hijacked by the Americans, or so the French claimed, and the youth culture was slow to appear. When the Beatles played at the Olympia music hall they got second billing, and in 1966 there was a scandal over a fleeting pop star named Antoine because he had long hair and sang in a *flowered* shirt.

I WAS LEARNING HOW CONSERVATIVE France is and how it prefers novelty to the new. There was so much to learn and I was free to do so at the *Herald Tribune,* one of the oldest newspapers in Paris (it was founded by James Gordon Bennett in 1887) and certainly the quirkiest. I began on the women's page, then wrote back-page features, more or less on what I wanted. Reporters have (or used to have) the salutary saying that today's news wraps tomorrow's fish: we are all in the ephemera trade, or were in less self-important days. Features are footnotes, a journalistic sideshow: sometimes they illuminate the main news, sometimes they relieve it. I learned that indirection was the best way to describe the complex society I was living in. I fled the quaint, was captivated by the unconsidered and found that by listening carefully and unobtrusively I could do interviews (shyness helped). It was like diving from the high board.

An early interview was with Eleanor Roosevelt who was kindness itself, but I had been born in FDR's presidency and could not believe I was sitting next to this noble woman at lunch in the Hotel Crillon, oddly entitled to quiz her. So I didn't, or did it very badly. I remember that at the end of our lunch she thriftily took the unfinished bottle of mineral water up to her hotel room. There were many interviews in Paris and in the rest of Europe, often with the celebrated, just as often with the unremarked, such as a headachy water dowser in the Vaucluse or an English truck driver seeking to grow the world's largest pumpkin. England was a frequent source, its unframed countryside providing relief from France's municipal marigolds and rows of pollarded trees, its writers and artists at home in the world outside their workrooms, its eccentrics cheerful, ungrudging and definitely not Cartesian.

The French belief that they encapsulate the clarity and reason of a seventeenth-century philosopher is befuddling but, as a historian says, it seems as if the French were always Cartesian, even before Descartes. Only foreigners wonder at how a people can at once be so rational and so unreasonable: an American artist who had known France since the 1920s said in an interview, "The French are so logical they don't even make sense." Of course, Descartes wrote in French, rather than the expected Latin or Greek, thus enshrining the other article of French secular belief, the genius of the French language.

That unyielding reason and unchanging language could be so important in modern life—and the many bellyflops that occurred as a result—led to smiles and subjects for columns, but to someone from the loose-limbed and careless USA there is also something admirable in a belief in order and measure, however elusive. And what an epiphany to find it, as Henry James did in 1870: "From Nice to Boulogne I was deeply struck with the magnificent order and method and decency and prosperity of France—with the felicity of *manner* in all things—the completeness of form."

COMPLETENESS OF FORM IS EVIDENT in the very shape of France, not comic like Italy or overblown like the USA: *l'hexagone,* tidy but diverse. If in American grade schools geography is quickly dispensed with, in bounteous France it is a source of pride and serious study. "Did geography invent France?" asked the historian Fernand Braudel in his last book, *L'Identité de la France,* and answered yes. The hexagon is the heart of France, Paris merely its head. Every Parisian claims rural roots, real or imagined, and it is fashionable to become mayor of the village where one has a country house. If the French are disunited as a people—one and divisible, a historian says—and held in check only by an unyielding army of civil servants who treat them as potential threats to the established order rather than as citizens, they are united by the single word *France.*

The French know they are imperfect—or to be more accurate each French person knows that all other French persons are imperfect—and they are quick to say that *les français* (i.e., everyone else) are *changeants* and *individualistes* (fickle and self-centered). I learned from writing about them that the French like being teased: They always think someone else is the target. But no one makes light of France.

The idea is that France is somehow better than the French. Braudel, writing of the sunny and flower-filled spring of 1940 before the Germans came, says that defeated France was not the true France, which always survives its own history. *La douce France* of the hexagon remains its gentle self even when its citizens are killing each other as they so often have—the seventeenth-century religious wars, the Revolution, the Commune, the Occupation and the vengeful *épuration* (purge) that followed—in its name. "This realm," said François Mauriac, "is always being delivered from itself."

France is a person, a woman. "Ah! Mother, such as we are we are here to serve you," Charles de Gaulle wrote during the war, and when he died in 1970 his successor, Georges Pompidou, proclaimed that France is a widow, giving the general's end an oddly oedipal cast.

THESE DAYS THE HEXAGON SEEMS to be getting ready to be a part of a greater community, its aloofness tempered by the market, by politics that have become more consensual than contestatory and, perhaps, simply by travel that has opened minds and improved manners. When I first came here, people would swiftly close the elevator door in my face rather than share the ride; today they hold the door open and say *bonjour.* They used to condemn American culture, shoes and food. Now they deconstruct Disney, jog in Nikes, consume 274,000 hamburgers a day, and put fish between slices of bread.

It hasn't come easily—the French buy more tranquilizers and mood medicines than any other Europeans—and one enduring battlefield, reduced now to minor skirmishes, is the French language. In 1998 it was announced that as there are now several woman cabinet ministers, they could be addressed as *Madame la Ministre,* but one doesn't change the sex of a noun without the permission of the Académie Française. The academy's perpetual secretary fired off a letter to the president of the republic referring to the change as an affair of state and all France laughed. "Let Us Liberate the French Language," urged *Le Monde.* Times have changed.

The debate on the sex of a *ministre* occurred just as France was launching a massive commemoration of the student uprising thirty years earlier when even the idea of a female minister would have seemed outlandish. Whole sections of bookstores were devoted to studies of 1968, newspapers reproduced pages from the time, the student leader Daniel Cohn-Bendit ("Dany le Rouge") was endlessly interviewed, his red hair now tarnished by time, his charisma intact. "I was the clown, the prankster of '68," he said. He was that and more: the wide-eyed rebel who dared say "Why?" to authority, who gave youth and factory workers fleeting hope, who terrified the establishment from Gaullists to Communists, although he never threatened violence or sought power for himself. In a country stifled by conformity, he was a genial lord of misrule.

When one thinks of the horrors of 1968—the gunning down of Martin Luther King, Robert Kennedy and the students in Mexico City, the rage and sorrow that Vietnam, Biafra and Prague evoked—it seems amazing that the events in Paris captured world headlines, especially since they ended so quickly: the government lifted restrictions on gas and everyone got into their cars and went off for the long Whitsun weekend during which seventy people died in road accidents while, by official count, only one had died in the uprising.

De Gaulle, it is true, resigned a few months later, but he was replaced by Georges Pompidou, a Gaullist who vowed that things would never be the same and then did his best to make sure they were.

I loved the May *événements,* as the French called them, the exhilaration, the solidarity, the crude and powerful posters printed by Beaux Arts students who had finally stopped drawing Doric columns, and the night when Cohn-Bendit, the French-born son of a German refugee father, was thrown out of France and thousands chanted, *Nous sommes tous des Juifs Allemands,* We are all German Jews.

I admired the *Préfet de Police,* or police chief, of Paris, Maurice Grimaud, who tried to reason with the panicky government, who did his unsuccessful best to curb police violence, and who had three children fighting on the student barricades. But mostly I was having too good a time during *les événements* to write much about them, and for all the new studies I am not sure there is any conclusion to be drawn. It was not a revolution, says the historian Pierre Nora: "the event was its own event . . . and is still referred to as 'the events of May 1968,' as though no other designation were possible."

There was, I think, a change because May extended the hexagon's psychological cordon sanitaire to include *les marginaux,* or those on the edge. Widened margins meant that someone who marched to a different drummer wasn't necessarily an outcast; he could become a government minister or the personal physician of the president of the republic. Christian de Portzemparc, who in his Beaux Arts days in the late 1960s read Foucault and Barthes and studied the films of Godard and Antonioni instead of the official curriculum, could in 1994 become the first Frenchman to win the Pritzker prize, always referred to as the architect's Nobel.

Pierre Nora's remarks on 1968 appear in a series he edited called *Les Lieux de Mémoire* (The Realms of Memory), in which historians examined the changing attitudes to and uses of such indelible symbols as Verdun, the Marseillaise, the French language, Joan of Arc and Descartes. "The very dynamics of commemoration have been turned around," Nora wrote in his conclusion in 1992. "The memorial model has triumphed over the historical model and ushered in a new, unpredictable and capricious view of the past. . . . What matters is not what the past imposes on us but what we bring to it."

Until recently, memory in France seemed to mean formal commemoration, which can be a form of concealment. Then questions began to be asked about the meaning of French identity and memory. The feeling for the *terroir,* literally France's earth, became mere nostalgia by the 1970s, when fewer than 10 percent of the population were working the land and housing projects were sprouting on the edges of cities. The influx of *pieds noirs* from Algeria and of foreign immigrants meant that Frenchness had to be rethought. Above all, the evasions of the Occupation had finally to be addressed.

The painful process began with *The Sorrow and the Pity,* the documentary about resistance and betrayal that Marcel Ophuls made in 1969 for government-controlled French television, which refused to show it. It got limited cinema release instead, and the night I saw it the audience left the movie house stupefied and silent. It was followed, less successfully, in 1973 by an eight-hour documentary about France from World War I to the Algerian war made by Ophuls's producers, André Harris and Alain Sedouy, and called *Français, Si Vous Saviez* (Frenchmen, If Only You Knew). The French have long been lied to and their own complicity in these lies prevents them from facing the truth, Harris said in an interview. The French are self-satisfied and thus easily duped, said Sedouy.

The same year Robert O. Paxton's *Vichy France* was translated, followed by *Vichy France and the Jews,* implacably researched revelations of the extent of French collaboration. If it took an American to open French eyes, soon French historians of all political leanings took on the subject, and by the mid-1980s I had a file labeled "French Memory." As I look at the file now, it tells me less than I thought it would, although perhaps the label was sufficient: France could no longer erase a past in which the eager participation of civil servants and ordinary citizens made it possible for the undermanned Germans to accomplish their dreadful task.

The French already knew much of what they were finally learning; perhaps it has become easier to live with now that most of those responsible are as dead as their mouthless victims. That François Mitterrand had been a Vichy functionary as well as a resistant was hardly news. Nor was the fact that Maurice Papon, the zealous servant of Vichy finally brought to trial for crimes against humanity fifty-two years after the war's end, had been minister of the budget under Valéry Giscard d'Estaing, the leader of a parliamentary commission named by Georges Pompidou, and Maurice Grimaud's predecessor as Paris police chief, appointed by de Gaulle and responsible for the beating and disappearance in 1961 of still-uncounted numbers of Algerians during their war for independence.

In the spring of 1998 a French government survey revealed that 58 percent of the French considered themselves racist or somewhat racist and that 59 percent thought there were too many Arabs in France. A few weeks later, a predominantly black and brown-skinned French football team won the World Cup and there was a shameless about-face as the nation praised its "multi-culturism." Even Charles Pasqua, who as minister of the interior had been rigidly against immigrants, suggesting they be returned to their countries in chartered planes, now said they should stay and be given residents' cards. And 50 percent of the French population agreed. A further, and probably temporary, widening of margins. "When France is strong she can be generous," Pasqua said.

Perhaps Gertrude Stein got it right in *Paris France* when she wrote that the most important things to the French are logic and fashion. By fashion she did not mean clothes but "the real thing in abstraction," something that changes while the fundamentals remain. In other words something that allows the French to be *changeant* without falling into qualms or contradiction. She was writing in 1939 to make Americans love France, just as Edith Wharton had done in 1919 with *French Ways and Their Meaning*. Wharton was masterly at taking such hurdles as French rudeness in a stately leap:

"The French often economise manners as they do francs. The discovery is disillusioning until one goes back to its cause, and learns to understand that, in a society based on caution and built about an old and ineradicable bureaucracy, obsequiousness on the one side is sure to breed discourtesy on the other."

After so many years, I suppose I know France somewhat but I understand it not at all. Everything has its contrary: the day you are so fed up you want to pack your bags there will be a sudden giggle with a stranger over something you both saw in the street; for de Gaulle's plaint about the impossibility of governing a country with 265 cheeses there is Thomas Moore's, "Who can help loving a country that has taught us six hundred and eighty-five ways to dress eggs?"

Loving France does not mean loving one's own land less (I love mine a lot more than when I left it). I have never met anyone who can bear the word *expatriate,* with what Martha Gellhorn called its seedy decayed sound. If leaving your native land means transferring your roots to a shallower soil, in that shallower soil lie the mysteries, constraints and delights of a new quotidian.

Early in my stay here, in 1964, there was a debate in the old American Center on the boulevard Raspail between prewar and postwar Americans in Paris. The prewar group was stunning: Man Ray, the composer Virgil Thomson, the *New Yorker's* Janet Flanner and Maria Jolas who, with her husband, edited the literary magazine *transition* from a house in Colombey-les-Deux-Eglises later bought by Charles de Gaulle. Janet Flanner began by remarking, "No one stays at home voluntarily," and then people said why they had come and what they had found.

"I discovered it was delightful to be a foreigner, not only could I start with a fresh viewpoint but I was pardoned many faults I wouldn't have been," Man Ray said. "Some came for financial reasons, some came for the ride," said Maria Jolas. "Others came because of Prohibition, which created a rather disagreeable atmosphere for the lighthearted."

Of course they had come to France in a time of unparalleled creativity. "One could sense that here was the rare moment of the century," Mrs. Jolas said. "I knew the minute I hit France in 1921 that it was a magic time," said Virgil Thomson. "It's nice to be in a magic place in a magic time."

The magic time was already long past, but then Maria Jolas mentioned an article in a 1932 issue of *transition* on why Americans live in Paris. Gertrude Stein's reply is the one that endures: "It isn't so much what France gives you as what it doesn't take away."

PARIS FRANCE

WHEN PARIS
PUT ON ITS BEST DRESS

PARIS—It is nice to think of dressing up and smelling rose petals at a time of year when everyone is taking off his and her clothes and the pervasive perfume, if it can be called that, is Ambre Solaire.

The best dressing-up occurred in Paris between the two world wars. The occasions were costume balls of ravishing elegance. Prince Jean-Louis de Faucigny-Lucinge, who attended all of them and gave two with his late wife, Baba, a noted beauty, has described some of the better parties in his book, *Fêtes Mémorables: Bals Costumés*.

The French have been dressing up for centuries. What makes the 1920s and 1930s so particular, Lucinge says, is that it was a period when society and bohemia joined in a brief and happy mix.

"A congregation of what is called *gens du monde* and painters, poets, writers, artists—it was a mixture that created the event. Let us say Picasso would have done the decor, Valentine Hugo the costumes, Georges Auric the music, Lacretelle or Cocteau or Morand would have written a little scenario."

There would be three or four balls, for about two hundred guests, each season between April and July. Ideally they would be held outdoors, like the Faucigny-Lucinge Second Empire ball in June 1934, in the Bois de Boulogne, which ended at dawn with romantically costumed young couples rowing on the lake.

The most assiduous partygoers and party throwers were Count Etienne de Beaumont and his wife, satirized by Radiguet in *Le Bal du Comte d'Orgel* and creators of the Bal Louis XIV, the Bal de la Mer, the Bal des Tableaux Célèbres and one based on the fairy tales of Perrault to which seventeen-year-old Johnny Lucinge was invited as Prince Charming by a friend of his mother.

The boy was dazzled by the beauty of the costumes and by the appearance of his host, dressed in pink tights and tiny wings as Cupid. "He liked making appearances. Sometimes he would change his costume three or four times a night," Lucinge says.

For sheer magnificence the greatest party giver after the Beaumonts was Carlos de Bestegui, whose Venetian fete at the Palazzo Labia in 1951 was the last great ball. Lucinge's publisher insisted that he include later fetes, such as the Rothschild Proust ball and the Hélène Rochas "My Fair Lady" ball, but for Lucinge these were just collections of show biz and jet-set celebs. The party, he says, is over.

But when it was still going on, what larks! The theme would be announced several months in advance so that costumes could be made and invitiations be argued over (the people one invited to costume balls were not necessarily the ones one would have dinner with). The most important part was the guest's arrival, or entrée, for which he or she might have commissioned an aubade by Poulenc or a verse by Cocteau. Sometimes guests included professional dancers in their entrées and underwent a training pro-

Coco Chanel and Fulco di Verdura, Second Empire Ball, 1934.
Roger-Viollet

gram to be able to keep in step. Although Elsa Maxwell once came as Napoléon III and the bearded Christian Bérard as Little Red Riding Hood, travesties were not the thing. The point was, quite simply, to look marvelous. And everyone did.

To record the evening such photographers as Horst and Man Ray would snap individuals or groups. Among the inevitable beauties at each ball were Lady (Iya) Abdy who, says Cecil Beaton, invented size, being over six feet tall, the Duchess de Gramont, Baba de Lucinge, Countess Jean de Polignac, Princess Natalie Paley and Daisy Fellowes. Chanel attracted attention among the frills of the Second Empire ball by wearing black widow's weeds and attended another party dressed as a tree.

"She adored dressing up," Lucinge says. "She was at every party and disguised herself wonderfully. It amused her, she was at the height of her glory and started going out a lot and she absolutely loved it. She took great trouble and it was always very well done because she had her own ateliers."

It was also the time when colorful revues flourished in Paris so there were many theatrical costumers near Montmartre where guests could rent costumes. Some went to great expense, while Man Ray appeared in a rayon laundry sack whose corners he had cut out for his arms and legs and carried an egg beater in one hand. The Surrealist Roland Penrose attended another ball dressed as the clock that struck at the moment Tristam Shandy was conceived.

Lucinge says he and his wife loved the planning. One of their more brilliant strokes as a young married couple was a Proust ball in 1928, only six years after the author's death. Many of Proust's friends attended and one was only narrowly persuaded not to impersonate the Master himself. The Lucinges came as the Marquis and Marquise de Saint-Loup, their costumes designed by the painter Jean Hugo whose wife, Valentine, excelled at party costumes. The party ended at 6 A.M. under the Eiffel Tower but usually they ended earlier, Lucinge says.

"People had taken such trouble to dress and prepare themselves that sometimes they weren't very comfortable and they were so excited about appearing that by two in the morning they were tired out. It never lasted terribly late."

One party where Lucinge and several other guests were extremely uncomfortable was the Bal des Matières given by the Vicomte and Vicomtesse de Noailles in 1929, at which guests were asked to wear costumes of strange materials. Charles de Noailles wore an impeccable tailcoat in oil cloth, Lucinge was a knight in paper armor designed by Valentine Hugo. "It was rather coarse packing paper. I hated it. I disliked the look of it, I disliked the look of it on myself and it was very uncomfortable. I was pleased on no account."

For the same ball, the writer Maurice Sachs pondered on whether to wear feathers or furnishing fabrics and decided instead to cover himself in pebbles, causing his dancing partners considerable discomfort. "I should have worn shells," he later wrote.

Part of the attraction of costume balls, Lucinge says, was that they gave people a chance both to play another role and to be themselves at their best. It is touching to imagine this highly sophisticated world filled for one evening with childlike excitement and a sort of innocence.

"Absolutely," Lucinge says, "and it was innocent, which is a very strange thing, because a lot of those people were more than sophisticated and yet they enjoyed themselves like children." After 1936, he says, the feeling that Europe was heading toward tragedy changed the party mood.

Even Maurice Sachs asked himself if the enjoyment of such pleasures was morally justifiable, was it right to spend such vast sums for a single night? He concluded that what he would like would be to go to the parties and not think of such things.

The parties were frivolous, of course, but frivolity is no bad thing—it has been called play at its most evolved—and it should not be confused with triviality. The costume balls celebrated the ephemeral, which is a highly sophisticated way of celebrating life.

It was a brief moment when everything was important, and nothing. "My big regret," Lucinge says today, "is that Picasso wanted to do my wife's portrait and you know how it is when one is young, one says *tant pis*, another day.

"I was young and I was lightheaded, and the painting was never done."

August 3, 1987

MEN WILL BE BOYS

PARIS—Many tourists are disappointed by two of Paris's major attractions: the *Mona Lisa* and the French man. Nothing can be done about the *Mona Lisa,* but French men can now go to charm school. The first such course opened recently in Paris and it is called Alluring Boy.

"We thought of calling it 'Gentlemen' but we decided that wouldn't do," said the founder, Mag Pique, a blonde ex-model who also runs a modeling school for women.

It takes only three months and $120 to become an Alluring Boy. Although the course is barely a month old, thirty would-be A.B.s have signed up.

Students learn how to dress, how to speak, how to eat asparagus, foie gras and lobster, how to carve chicken or open champagne, how to break dates and how to make friends.

They are taught to offer women cigarettes, to kiss their hands, to rise when they approach or leave a table and to carry their packages. When they travel by car they are told to be courteous and sportive, when they travel by air they are advised not to tell their neighbors about recent crashes.

One can scarcely wait for the first group of Alluring Boys to graduate.

The present class includes a few men who want training as models or *cover-boys,* as they are called in French, but the majority are socially mobile employees in search of *savoir-vivre.*

"We have salesmen, executives and an *attaché de presse,*" said Mme Mag. "We have only four or five in a class because they get paralyzed if there are more. They are much shyer than women."

Toward the end of the course the Alluring Boys will hear lectures on diet, skin care and civil law. At the moment they are in the hands of Marc Cadiot, whose field is applied psychology, and the Marquis Franco Fabris di Favaro, who gives tuition in dress, protocol, ease and allure.

The marquis, a handsome Venetian *cover-boy,* was wearing an outfit only an Alluring Boy cum laude could carry: a deep green double-breasted and narrow-waisted blazer with socks to match, ox-blood buckled moccasins and trousers in a window-pane plaid.

Between the marquis's sock and elegantly crooked trouser leg no skin showed. Between Mr. Cadiot's sock and trouser was a patch of white.

"You are showing skin," Mme Mag gaily admonished her psychologist. He blushed.

"There are certain cases in which short socks are perfectly correct," said the marquis politely.

"The marquis's work complements mine," said Mr. Cadiot, uncrossing his legs. "Once a man knows how to dress and eat he is partly rid of his blocks.

"We are dealing with personal problems of social adaptation,"

Mr. Cadiot continued. "Our students are coming into or are in a milieu that is not their own."

In the process of social orientation, the Alluring Boys learn how to become the leader of a group in ten minutes, how to avoid arguments and how to acquire assurance. In some cases psychoanalysis is advised, but most students have the same basic problem:

"Women," said Mr. Cadiot. "If they want to shine, it is because of women."

The gloss comes from the marquis, who is very earnest. He tells his students what to read ("I don't suggest Proust right away—that would be silly"), what movies and plays to see, where to eat, how to decorate their flats, when to send flowers and what to do with their hands.

"Men learn fast," said the marquis. "They are more disciplined than women."

Mme Mag, the marquis and Mr. Cadiot agree that *savoir-vivre* is within the reach of anyone who truly wants to be an Alluring Boy.

What is *savoir-vivre?* "I prefer to call it *savoir-être*," said Mme Mag. "It has the very precise sense of following the social conventions of a certain milieu," said Mr. Cadiot.

"It means being nice to everyone," said the marquis, "from the baroness to the concierge."

"Especially the concierge," said Mme Mag.

December 15, 1965

GENÊT:
FRENCH RIGOR AND AMERICAN GUSTO

PARIS—In 1922 *Ulysses* was published. So were *The Waste Land, The Forsythe Saga, The Beautiful and Damned* and *The Enormous Room,* to say nothing of *The Garden Party* and *Peter Whiffle.* It was a year when apparently everyone was young and in Paris, and Janet Flanner, mad on dancing and filled with literary ambition, arrived in a hotel on the rue Bonaparte.

Before Paris she had written a New York–based novel called *The Cubical City,* which was, she says, not good as its title, and before that she had been a film critic in her native Indianapolis, which had the first movie palace with an orchestra that rose and fell.

The crucial moment in Miss Flanner's career occurred three years after she arrived in Paris when Harold Ross, whom she had met in New York, invited her to write a Paris letter for his new magazine, the *New Yorker.* Ross instructed her to write about what the French thought was going on, not what she thought was going on, and gave her an inexplicable pen name: Genêt.

From the start, the Letter from Paris ranged spaciously and stylishly over politics, the arts, personalities and gossip with a scope no other journalist can touch. Cabled fortnightly to New York, it was topical in intent ("I used to beat *Time* magazine. That made me laugh") but has proved to be enduring literature, as enlightening to the Paris-based reader as to the little old lady in Dubuque.

"I like the Paris Letter, I think in the *New Yorker* it is a useful vehicle," Miss Flanner says. "It's quite bearded and antique now," she adds.

When she began the Letter she knew she wanted it to be "precisely accurate, highly personal, colorful and ocularly descriptive.

"The speed can be lifted to such a high tension in it. It's an animated picture frame, it's very animated. I don't have to try to animate it."

Miss Flanner is small, striking and doughty, a constant smoker and an elegant and salty talker. She wishes her skull were shaped like her friend Mary McCarthy's, and she used her nose as a pretext to avoid the stage career her mother intended for her: "I pointed out that with this nose I'd be playing Juliet's nurse or Juliet's nurse's nurse, and never Juliet." An early photograph of her peering, like Eustace Tilley, through a monocle, and another portrait, from Horst's *Salute to the Thirties* (for which she wrote a charming preface), in which she gazes plaintively into the middle distance, suggest that she has had moments of taking herself rather seriously.

She has always lived in hotel rooms (currently, the Paris Ritz). "I am very undomestic. And I don't want one of those jewels of a French cook who want to cook a little and eat a lot."

There is no journalistic disorder in the room; there are no files. "I have a pretty stocky memory, after all," Miss Flanner says. She also relies heavily on the *New Yorker*'s library.

"The *New Yorker* has a honey of a library full of checkers checking. All those people are experts. Hardly any writer is protected like that. It gives me a feeling of being pleasantly goaded."

These days Janet Flanner spends more and more time in the United States, though she has yet to go back home to Indiana ("not on your life, baby"). She filed her last words on Gen. de Gaulle from Napa Valley, where her younger sister lives, fording a flooded stream to get to the telegrapher's. She appears on talk shows and is the subject of a long television documentary now being made. "I hope I'll live through it," she says. "I'll never have enough clothes to live through it."

Two collections of Letters from Paris have been published, and this past Bastille Day a new volume of, for the most part, lighter snippets from 1925 to 1939 came out under the title "Paris Was Yesterday." It is, Miss Flanner says, the first of her books to sell well, but she doesn't quite approve of it and had to be nudged into letting it come out.

"I'm rather old-fashioned and stuffy. This isn't the type of the *New Yorker* at all—it's rather giddy and flip."

It is a marvelously high-spirited book. "So much has been going on in Paris that you wouldn't believe it, even if we merely claimed to have witnessed half of it," one Letter begins. The book has its sober moments but it rejoices in such characters as the exquisite Jacques Hennessey, "who never walked if the effort took him away from carpets"; Marguerite Long, "an obedient and powerful French pianist popular in ministerial circles"; Mata Hari, who was half Dutch and half Javanese ("both sides predominated, giving her the benefit of neither"); and Dr. Bougrat, "one of the most popular poisoners of Marseilles, recently fled from his cell to Caracas, where he enjoys a flourishing general practice though nose and throat were his original specialty."

The title "Paris Was Yesterday" makes no sense at all, Miss Flanner says, but it is provocative. It also implies, with some justice, that Paris is not today.

"It certainly does not improve. As for those baby skyscrapers they're building up the river, they really are revolting little things."

Recently, an American asked Miss Flanner why she was so nostalgic for the 1920s. "Number one, I was fifty years younger, which is very attractive. Number two, Paris was fifty years older, which is also attractive."

When she began her Letter from Paris, Janet Flanner thought of Gibbon as a model; Pater and Browning also helped. She spent a year in Berlin before coming to Paris and during the 1930s wrote the Letter from London for a spell, but the overwhelming influence on her style came from living in France. "The critical faculty, taste. That's what I have learned here. That and precision of language."

The result is prose that can sound, uniquely, as if it came straight from the *grand siècle,* at once sonorous and succinct. There is American gusto but there is also French rigor, and above all there is the very French combination of pure reason mixed with melodrama. She is at her best on extravagant subjects: Isadora Duncan, French murderers, Gen. de Gaulle.

"I am very sympathetic to anyone who's historically an exception. De Gaulle's got such a damn good mind. We don't often get a president of our republic with such a good mind—you and I don't."

Miss Flanner loves Chartres for its candy and its cathedral ("I'm very interested in ecclesiastical architecture, remarkably for an old Indiana Quaker"). She likes Italian ice cream, French fresh vegetables, hates it if someone says "hi," and says the reason she is at the Ritz is for its nearby trees.

"I am a dendrophile. So is my dear sister, Hildegarde. She is a poet." For so urbane a person, she loves country pleasures. "I like country things. I like quiet. I'm very fond of sunsets. I'm not an expert on them, but I like them quite well."

She works extremely hard. "Anyone who works as hard as I do has to be a good writer. I work with a conscientious kind of discipline. I work like a beaver, I go over each Letter for clarification, for mining, for a spot of gold."

On her desk there are sheets of paper bearing the thrifty letterhead of some foreign correspondents' association and covered with her large, rolling hand. A small Olivetti perches on the desk corner. Janet Flanner turned eighty last spring, but she is an unflagging enthusiast.

"I love writing. I'm just nuts on writing," she says. "Just give me an inkpot and paper and pen, and away I go."

September 6, 1972

THE FRIENDS OF MONA LISA

*La Gioconda is, in the truest sense, Leonardo's masterpiece,
the revealing instance of his mode of thought and work. . . .
Certainly Lady Lisa might stand as the embodiment of the
old fancy, the symbol of the modern idea.*

WALTER PATER, 1869

PARIS—In fact, the *Mona Lisa,* or *La Joconde,* as the French call
her, might stand for anything, and does. She can be found advertising everything from grapes to condoms, parodying politicans
from Mao to John Major, decorating beaded curtains found in
Vietnam and a cookie jar made in USA.

She is the most famous artwork in the world. The space surrounding her bulletproof frame is the noisiest in the Louvre, with
people jostling as they might to see a celebrity, which she is. "She
has an enormous recognition factor, she is like a top model. A top
model that costs nothing and thus an image that expresses nothing, or anything," says Jean Margat, a retired geologist and probably the world's leading jocondophile.

Margat is the president of Les Amis de Mona Lisa, a group of
about forty fans and collectors that held its annual meeting last

Saturday with members seated around a U-shaped table and clutching wrapped items that they had found during the year for the show-and-tell that would follow the president's and treasurer's reports. It was the group's tenth anniversary, feted by a Mona Lisa champagne and a reproduction in nougatine and marzipan that proved very tricky to cut.

Mona Lisa collectors aren't daft and dull like people who collect Camembert labels or key rings; they cannot be greedy because so many new items constantly appear that all notions of value and investment opportunities vanish. Unlike most collectors, they are having fun: one might—one must—say they are jocund.

Among active members (Pierre Rosenberg, the Louvre's director, is an honorary member) are a couple of engineers, painters, a bookbinder, a Dutch librarian, a postal employee also interested in collecting Chaplin, Coca-Cola and aubergines, and Bruno Figueroa, the press attaché of the Mexican embassy who presented the prize exhibit, a huge collage representing the theft of the *Mona Lisa* in 1911 and its recovery two years later, after Picasso and Apollinaire had been falsely implicated in the foul deed.

The unveiling of the collage was greeted by oohs and bravos while Figueroa, in his Mexican-made black Mona Lisa T-shirt, blushed. The work had its origins in his wife's complaints about the clutter caused by his collection, solved by its being composed into the collage that will hang in his embassy office.

Other applauded offerings were coffee mugs decorated with a mustached Mona Lisa in imitation of Marcel Duchamp's 1919 spoof (the mustache disappears when hot liquid is poured into the mug) and Russian matriochka dolls in which the outer one represents La Joconde while those nested inside are various representations of the Virgin Mary. "A good example of the frequent confusion of the Mona Lisa and the Madonna," Jean Margat observed.

The painting has been analyzed by everyone from Freud to Camille Paglia ("I think that what Mona Lisa is ultimately saying is that males are unnecessary"). Her expression has been ascribed

to pregnancy, syphilis and jaundice. Her popularity, Margat says, comes from the worldwide publicity surrounding the 1911 theft, which was even covered in comic strips, followed by Duchamp's celebrated outrage which opened the way to further transgressions, acceptable because there has always been something a bit transgressive about the lady herself (is she, for example, Leonardo in drag, as has been suggested?).

Margat became interested in the 1950s when such friends as the writer-musician Boris Vian stuck pins in Mona Lisa's face. As a variation on Raymond Queneau's *"Exercises de Style,"* he began collecting and in 1959 produced a famous issue of the magazine *Bizarre,* devoted to the *Mona Lisa.* Since then, her image has grown exponentially. (The meetings of Les Amis de Mona Lisa must be the only ones in the world in which the word *exponentially* is on everyone's lips.)

There have been two Margat-inspired Mona Lisa shows recently: one last summer in Geneva, where it was funded by Swiss banks, and one in Brittany in 1996, where the local prefect banned the show's poster on moral grounds because it showed Mona Lisa smoking a joint.

Some members found themselves involved almost by accident. René Royer, the retired bookbinder, became intrigued when he saw pictures of Mona Lisa in profile, Sophie Bouvard, who is unemployed, saw an ad for chocolate bars imagining Mona Lisa full length. Then she started seeing her everywhere—on shoeboxes, tulip bulbs, chocolate in Greece, pantyhose in Brazil. For this year's meeting she compiled a list of ninety-five French *départements* where jocondophiles can find a reference, from Mona Lisa pizzerias to a discotheque, hairdressers and real estate promoters.

There is a Paris bookstore whose business has soared since it called itself Mona Lisait. A favorite jocondophile anagram is *On m'a sali* (I've been defiled). At Saturday's meeting, from 9:30 in the morning to 5 P.M., the club's members traded, admired and were unusually uncompetitive. A couple of heavy leather scrapbooks circulated showing references to the *Mona Lisa,* including: an article on dental implants, news from an agriculture show in central France that a heifer named Joconde had won a prize, and a 1993 dispatch from *Le Progrès de Lyon* concerning a New Jersey family that owns a *Mona Lisa* given to one of their ancestors by Marie-Antoinette. The New Jersey version is ten years younger and more elegant than the one in the Louvre, the correspondent said.

The actual history of the painting—"the mortal whose divine gaze triumphs over sightless gods," as André Malraux typically put it—is of less interest to jocondophiles than what has been done with it. "The history of the woman is not nearly as fascinating," says René Royer. And the painting itself?

"I've seen it only once. It was a big disappointment," Bruno Figueroa said.

October 25, 1997

A RUEFUL GLANCE AHEAD
AT NEW FACE OF PARIS

PARIS—Like the city itself, the street names of Paris offer every pleasure: poetic (rue du Cherche-Midi), intimate (twenty-three street names begin with the word "*petit[e]*"), military (thirteen are named after colonels and sixty-four after generals from Anselin to Zarapoff), bucolic (rue des Petits-Champs), literary (Voltaire alone has given his name to a boulevard, street, quai, *cité* and *impasse*, dead end), spiritual (rue de l' Assomption) and criminal (rue des Mauvais-Garçons).

Poets sing the streets of Paris, tourists buy reproductions of blue street signs. All Paris history is there in a name, so think of what it must be like to live on a street named AW15.

An American photographer named John Schults and his French wife, Bernadette, and their neighbors in a new housing complex have lived on Voie AW15, or AW15 road, in central Paris for two years—a name so improbable and so tentative sounding that taxi drivers won't go near it and even the local tax man doesn't want to take Mr. Schults's money because Voie AW15 does not appear on his official lists.

For the same reason the local police station didn't want to renew Mr. Schults's residence permit, and presents for Mr. Schults's children that were guaranteed Christmas delivery last year finally arrived on Jan. 4 and March 11.

"No mail order house wants to deal with us," Mr. Schults says. While awaiting a permanent name, Voie AW15 was not even given a temporary street sign, so no one can find it.

"When you leave the Métro, you'll pass the *tabac* and the photo lab on rue de la Procession, which means you're getting close. Watch out for the railway bridge and then . . .." Mr. Schults's voice trails off. "Usually I just tell people to telephone when they get to the neighborhood and I come down and meet them."

Voie AW15, which used to be near the now eradicated Passage Falguière, is one of several streets hewn out for the new housing and shopping complexes on the edge of the fourteenth and fifteenth arrondissements, where Montparnasse has been so profitably and ruthlessly modernized. Like other examples of modern Paris planning, it is a desolate sight.

While the big changes in the Paris cityscape grab the carping headlines—the Centre Pompidou, the Pei pyramid, the Opéra Bastille—it is the smaller changes that are slowly and irrevocably changing the face of Paris. Terrible new street lighting, concrete tubs of municipal marigolds, officious plastic arrows, the metal-and-plastic flower stalls that were once dark green wood, the electronic billboards dispensing useless information: These are the details that erode the whole.

Paris has always been the most ordered capital, now it is merely one of the most tidy. Its architects' visions of harmony and strength have degenerated into the dainty fidgeting of a house-proud *bourgeoise*. The finicky little changes that can be seen throughout Paris are meant to conceal the bankruptcy of its modern town planning; instead, they reveal it. Paris, the grandest of cities, is in danger of becoming neat and quaint.

Around Voie AW15, where Bernadette and John Schults live, a playground has been built of such rigidity that every inch bears the slide rule's imprint and no child would stop there to skylark. A garish stucco wall in pistachio and lavender is intended to cut the area off from a railway freight station (soon to be covered over and developed), and presumably the wall's patronizing raison d'être is to bring a little color into the drab lives of the Schultses and their neighbors. Part of the wall decoration features the unmistakably gawky figure of Jacques Tati, which made people think that the street would be named after the late screen comedian.

They were wrong.

Time passed and there was still no name. Voie AW15 is a continuation of rue Georges Pitard, a lawyer and Resistance hero who actually lived several kilometers away on rue Séguier. Other new streets between the playground and the Tati wall bear fresh signs to indicate that they honor Maurice Maignon (1822–90), who founded a Catholic workers' center in Montparnasse, and Georges Leclanche (1839–82), who invented an electric battery—an electric battery, not even *the* electric battery. And still Voie AW15 remained nameless.

"It's paved now, there are even accidents on it, but it has no name," Mr. Schults said. "We're in a kind of no-man's-land, that's what we're in."

Last January Mr. Schults read in a throwaway local newspaper that Voie AW15 was going to be named after André Gide. Excitedly, he called the local police station, which confirmed the news. Then he telephoned the *mairie* (town hall) of the arrondissement and was given a stiff denial: Certain groups had protested against a street being named after a person of such dubious morality. The street remained nameless.

The choice of Paris street names is obscure, not to say top

secret. An attempt to prise the planned name of Voie AW15 from the responsible city functionary met with unbreakable resistance ("I can tell you nothing"). The legislation on street names is however apparently easily breached: one rule is that no street can be named after a living person, but it has been announced in the newspapers that on her ninetieth birthday in a few weeks a street will be named for the actress Arletty in her native suburb of Courbevoie.

Final decisions on street names are made by the mayor of Paris and his board. Streets can be named after memorable historical events or after people whose celebrity is certain to endure, although, with such exceptions as John F. Kennedy and Charles de Gaulle, the celebrated people must have been dead at least five years.

New street names cannot cause confusion with existing streets, nor is it any longer permitted to debaptize parts of streets in order to give them new names, the latter invidious practice having in one year created 30 new street names without one centimeter of asphalt having been laid.

For decades municipal councilors have argued about street names. Little imagining that a street would ever be named after the inventor of *an* electric battery, a councillor wondered twenty years ago why such obscure figures as Abel Truchet, a painter, and Abbé Carton, founder of the Notre-Dame de Bon-Secours hospice, should be honored in the seventeenth and fourteenth arrondissements, respectively.

"Most of the street names of Paris evoke nothing, and are grotesque," said the municipal councilor, André Weil-Curiel. "You can't please God, the devil and his father," replied one of his colleagues, who had just been through the mill for trying to debaptize rue de Beaujolais, along the north side of the Palais Royal, in order to name it after the writer Colette.

Not only did this displease Beaujolais drinkers but it created confusion because there was already Rue Collette, named after a

heroic *facteur*, or mailman. The end result was to leave rue Collette and rue de Beaujolais alone and give a minuscule section of
pavement at the other end of the Palais Royal the name Place
Colette.

At least Colette actually lived on rue de Beaujolais. Marshal
Foch lived on rue de Grenelle and not on avenue Foch (formerly
avenue du Bois). Stendhal also lived on rue de Grenelle and not
on any of the three Paris thoroughfares named after him. George
Sand lived at neither rue George Sand nor Villa George Sand,
and André Gide lived on rue Vaneau and certainly not on Voie
AW15.

One week before the functionary in the Paris street names division refused to divulge the future name of Voie AW15, the magazine *L'Express* printed an article on building changes in Montparnasse. It included a street clearly marked André Gide. But still no
one living on Voie AW15 had received notice of a name change.

Then, on the afternoon of November 7, when Bernadette
Schults was coming home with an armful of groceries and dia-
pers, she saw a group of dark-suited men standing in the play-
ground near the garish Jacques Tati wall in ceremonial postures.
The only person she recognized was Finance Minister Edouard
Balladur, whom she was surprised to find in her neighborhood. In
time one of the dark-suited men got up on a podium and pro-
claimed that Voie AW15 would henceforth be called rue André
Gide. Applause. The plaque bearing the new name was unveiled.
More applause.

"Then the oddest thing happened," Mrs. Schults says. "Instead
of being fixed to a wall the plaque was on a stand. And when the
ceremony was over they draped the cover over the sign again and
took it away."

She hopes that when a suitably clean wall is found the sign will
come back. In the meantime, after two years in the no-man's-land
of Voie AW15 the Schultses and their neighbors feel they actually
exist. Or almost.

"I won't be sure until I see the plaque rue André Gide on the wall," Mrs. Schults says. Her three-and-a-half-year-old daughter is cautious, too, when asked where she lives. "Paris," is all she will volunteer.

December 2, 1987

THE LAST OLD-TIME
SOUP KITCHEN IN PARIS

PARIS—All over town restaurateurs are moaning about falling business. Last week, at the annual directors' meeting of the Soupe Populaire in the Saint Sulpice quarter of the Left Bank, the chairman noted that there were only about one-third as many customers as there were ten years ago, but no one was moaning.

"The ideal would be that no one comes at all, that no one would be in need," Jacques Toutain, the meeting's chairman and vice president of the Soupe, said.

The Soupe Populaire of the sixth arrondissement, founded in 1894, is the last old-style soup kitchen in Paris. There used to be twenty, one for each arrondissement, founded in a time when industrialization was driving people from the land into a city already crowded with the jobless and the poor. By World War I, seven hundred portions of soup were served daily in the sixth arrondissement with two policemen keeping the hungry in line.

Government legislation over the years has made the need for
soup kitchens less urgent. The Soupe's remaining clients, as they
are respectfully called, are no longer pensioners and the temporarily distressed but hard-core vagabonds or *clochards,* who are
exempt from social benefits as they are from social constraints.

Between thirty and forty of them show up six days a week at
noon to down a hearty bouillon and a plain *plat du jour,* and they
are back on the street thirty minutes later. On Christmas and
New Year's Eve there is a special meal and a glass of wine. The
clients are always silent, sometimes courteous like the bleary-
eyed man who offered with a gesture to share his sausage and
lentils, sometimes abusive like the man who threw his tin dish at
Aline Janty, the cook. "Luckily I have quick reflexes," Mme Janty
said.

Mme Janty, however, has no wish to reform her clients; nor do
the volunteers from the bourgeoisie who clean up after them and
collect the token three francs clients pay, when they can, for the
meal. What is remarkable about the Soupe is the generosity of
spirit that prevails there: no condescension, no effusions of patronizing goodwill. A respect for privacy and grief is expressed in a
policy of anonymity laid down by the Soupe's longtime president,
Jean Guimont.

No questions are asked, no gratitude expected. No one is addressed by name although some clients have been coming for
years and there is no chat unless the client starts it. "I've had
them say they are just out of prison, it makes no difference to
me," M. Guimont said.

The Soupe is a tidy threadbare room at rue Clément with a
useful slot in its door for passersby to drop contributions. Plastic-
topped tables and benches line the room and at its end is an open
kitchen with two huge cauldrons from which Mme Janty and her
assistant dish up the soup. There is no decoration except for an

incongruous colorful painting of well-dressed people lined up for a catered buffet on a sunlit day outside the church of Saint-Germain-des-Prés. Labels identify the party goers as longtime members of the Soupe's board. No irony is intended and no offense taken: The clients in any case rarely look up from the floor when they enter or from their plates when they eat.

The Soupe's board is made up of neighborhood worthies who continue to come even when they have retired and moved to less fashionable areas. There is a diplomat's wife, a retired police inspector, the optician from rue Saint-Sulpice, a banker who manages the Soupe's small portfolio, a lawyer who negotiated the Soupe's lease, a retired official from the Finance Ministry and his wife, Roger Topolinski (the owner of the Lapérouse restaurant in the days when it was one of the best in Paris), and a former funeral director whose father began working with the Soupe in 1925 and who had in his pocket a list of funny stories to tell at the dinner that followed the meeting.

The moving spirit is Jean Guimont. "He is our father," Mme Janty said.

M. Guimont, always referred to as *le Président* although he is eighty-eight now and confined to his house, began working at the Soupe in 1936, recruited by his boss at the nearby Senate, where he was in charge of the budget. In turn, M. Guimont has brought in a much younger colleague from the Senate, Jacques Toutain, as vice president. "We do our best. Probably we make mistakes but we do care and we couldn't do more," M. Toutain said.

The Senate, the Institut de France and the Académie des Beaux-Arts, neighborhood institutions that might not be expected to care much about *clochards,* all help the Soupe out. Annual expenses and contributions just about balance at 300,000 francs (currently about $60,000). There are no fancy fund-raisers or charity balls. A nearby restaurant, La Foux, contributes food, and neighborhood butchers and bakers offer discount prices, but there are fewer butchers and bakers as rents rise. The patisserie on rue Saint-Sulpice that used to send over petits fours is now a boutique.

Not everyone is thrilled to have a soup kitchen in a high-rent area. Some time back, M. Guimont says, the building's owners opened eviction proceedings and went to the Cour de Cassation, or high court. The Soupe won.

At last week's annual board meeting, everyone sat on the Soupe's benches and the atmosphere was pleasantly amateur in both senses of the word, the first business of the day being to pass around a recent photograph of *le Président* to show how rosy and well he still looks. The last item on the agenda was the presentation of a medal to one of the board's longest-serving members, Dr. Charles Cachin. Dr. Cachin, it turned out, was unable to attend the meeting, which was just as well because M. Toutain had forgotten the medal.

In between, there was the treasurer's report, news of contributors—there was an appreciative hum when it was noted that Catherine Deneuve, who lives in the neighborhood, had given— and an expression of concern about the falling number of clients.

Perhaps clients should be given a warmer welcome, someone suggested. Perhaps the menu could be more varied. Perhaps there is too much competition from organizations like the *restaurants du coeur* founded by the late comedian Coluche and from the Petite Soeurs des Pauvres on rue Notre-Dame-des-Champs who dispense free sandwiches mornings until eleven o'clock.

"If they don't like the sandwiches, they throw them out and come here," one director said. Then, as in all restaurants, the usual litany of complaints about the customers began.

"We tried giving them apples but many of them have no teeth and threw them in the gutter."

"I offered one a Gauloise and he said no thanks, I only smoke Marlboros."

"I gave one a pastry and he said sorry, my doctors won't let me eat sugar." The plural doctors was much appreciated.

Affectionate joking over, the board went off to a dinner that M. Toutain had organized at the Senate. It ended with a toast to *le Président* and with the funeral director's amiable stories, and it consisted of trout filets in champagne sauce, magret de canard, cheese, savarin au rhum, and Muscadet and Bordeaux wines.

January 31, 1991

A STRUGGLE FOR THE SOUL
OF A PARIS RESTAURANT

PARIS—Culture and commerce clashed the other week at Le Balzar, the old and much loved Left Bank brasserie, and as is usual in France no one wanted to be on the side of commerce.

The occasion was an impassioned breakfast meeting at Balzar between the new owner, Jean-Paul Bucher, who specializes in enhancing the profit margins of old brasseries, and a newly constituted group of regulars called Les Amis du Balzar, who want to ensure that the restaurant does not change.

There was rumbling about the disappearance of cervelas sausage from the menu and the introduction of something called the marmite des pêcheurs, but for the most part the conversation was high-toned, concerned not with Balzar as a mere eatery but as a precious cultural heritage, what is called a *lieu de mémoire* like the Panthéon or the Lascaux caves.

An Alsatian, as by tradition many brasserie owners are, and a former chef, Bucher heads the Groupe Flo, a huge restaurant and catering chain with an annual turnover of over 1 billion francs and a plan to open in Beijing. His holdings include the Hippopotamus group and five restaurants at Disneyland, outside Paris, but he is most known for having taken over old Paris brasseries, beginning thirty years ago with Flo, speeding up the service and not necessarily improving the food. The most disappointing link in his chain is La Coupole, a financial success but a pleasure only to those who didn't know it before the takeover in 1989.

Le Balzar, off the boulevard St. Michel, is a lot smaller than La Coupole and has never been famous. The food is simple and robust, the ambience outstandingly welcoming: if one were dropped into Paris for just one meal, the choice would likely be lovable, unchanging Balzar. It has attracted celebrities from Deanna Durbin to François Mitterrand, but mostly has a core of neighborhood habitués who do not want such habits as lingering two hours over an omelette changed by a hard-nosed entrepeneur who might insist on rapid turnover or introduce—God forbid— frozen french fries.

And so when Bucher took over in April a group called Les Amis du Balzar was formed, and in late June they staged a dinnertime uprising, standing at their separate tables sharp at 9:30 P.M., according to *Le Figaro,* to protest the cultural heresy of the Groupe Flo's intrusion, to decry lowering standards, to express their soldarity with the staff and to demand, unsuccessfully, that Bucher be summoned at once on his mobile telephone. This was followed by an article in *Le Monde* referring to Bucher as a predator and speaking of escargots mummified by the deep freeze and an overcooked sea bass. Revolution was in the air.

"The Groupe Flo is powerful and unfortunately it is more than likely that they will destroy the Balzar spirit," says Lorenzo Valentin, a young publisher who leads Les Amis du Balzar. By now there are about five hundred Amis including a man who has

eaten at Balzar since he was two years old. The point of Les Amis is that Bucher is quite simply unfit to understand Balzar's cultural context. Some of them argue that a place belongs to those who use it and not only to the person who buys it and that Bucher should desist from running Balzar at all.

The breakfast meeting began with an air of unconvincing conviviality, Bucher ruddy and rich at the middle of a long table with the new manager of Balzar—cool and trim as a meat cleaver—at one end, and the anxious longtime chef at the other. In between were Les Amis telling Bucher he had to meet certain standards to keep their custom: "Do you want us still to come and what guarantees will you give to make us come?" asked Valentin.

"Look, we are here to understand each other," said Bucher (dubious glances). "It would be pity to take a small jewel like this which works perfectly well and transform it. I promise not to change it. Do you really think I need Balzar to make a living? I need to defend it along with you."

No one believed a word. How could a mere entrepreneur understand the need to linger over an omelette, find consolation on a bad day from an attentive waiter, and to rely on an unchanging menu (where *is* the cervelas?). It is a question of culture, not commerce, said Les Amis. His point exactly, said Bucher: had he not bought Balzar it would have become a McDonalds. (Not true, but why should such rhetorical devices as periphrastic exaggeration be the monopoly of Left Bank eggheads?)

Everyone, as is usual at French meetings, was talking at once. One woman's voice rose to describe a recent lunch with her eighty-three-year-old father at which she found her lamb chop inedible. Her credentials were impeccable: she and her father come at least once, sometimes twice, a week, her Dad likes his wine and the baba au rhum, and he is Alsatian. ("Ah, does he speak Alsatian?" inquired Bucher, trying to be friendly, which went down like a lead baba.) There are new dishes on the menu, the woman continued: can you certify that you do not use the Groupe Flo's kitchens?

Bucher stated that his restaurants have separate kitchens and called upon the chef who said he still deals with his suppliers and inspects each sole. "I cook with the same love I have had for thirty-three years and then there is that personal attack on my sea bass in *Le Monde*," he said bitterly.

For Valentin it was the *esprit* rather than the fish that mattered and expressing again his belief that the Flo group means the end of Balzar, he suggested that Bucher sell the restaurant. "I didn't buy it to sell it," Bucher replied shortly and remarked later that here he thought Les Amis had gone too far. They had also gone too far in suggesting that only they understood cultural memory.

"Why would I buy a little place like that, so small and special, if I didn't have the idea of cultural conservation? I fight for restaurants that have a history, I love them."

The meeting ended with Bucher agreeing to the conditions of Les Amis: no food from a centralized kitchen, respect for the personnel, the independence of Le Balzar. He further suggested that he hold monthly meetings with Les Amis to hear their views. "Trust me," he said, which they are not about to do. "An entrepreneur as rich as you is surrounded by flatterers, we do not flatter," said an ami virtuously. To an outsider it seemed sporting of him to have sat through two hours of insults and to have offered breakfast to boot.

"It was quite *sympathique*," he said later. "*Insupportable* but *sympathique*."

Les Amis are not reassured; for many of them Balzar is already lost and they fear greater changes when it reopens after the August recess, which begins this weekend. But, according to the chef, they can be sure of one thing: the cervelas will be back. It was just taken off the menu for the summer, he said, as it always has been.

August 8, 1998

PARIS IN A BOTTLE:
A WINE GROWER'S DREAM

PARIS—The merchants of Beaujolais are fueling trucks, hot-air balloons, private jets and other bandwagons to ensure the usual publicity-laden launch in mid-November of *Beaujolais Nouveau*. In the sterner vineyards of Burgundy and Bordeaux, the new wines are going through malolactics, or secondary fermentation, with everyone feeling chipper despite the threat of blocked sugar because of the summer's exceptional heat.

And near the Bastille in Paris, Jacques Mélac's 1989 vintage is about to begin its final vinification: Some thirty-five bottles will be taken out of his icebox, their contents filtered through coffee-machine paper, and a handsome label smacked on, Château Mélac.

Like so many wine châteaux, Château Mélac isn't really one. It is the rain gutter that runs along the first floor of Mélac's café on the rue Léon Frot in the eleventh arrondissement. There, facing southwest, flourishes a twenty-meter (sixty-five-foot) vine of hybrid baco grapes, which rounds the corner to a hairdresser on one side and a garage on the other. Each year, the grapes are harvested and made into Château Mélac.

Is this the vintage of the century? "Well, maybe," Mélac says doubtfully. He is lanky, with a huge cowcatcher mustache and a plump blond wife named Josiane.

And what are the characteristics of Château Mélac? Has it, perhaps, an intense core of peppery cassis flavors and a lingering aftertaste of violets? Is it medium-bodied, spicy and intense?

"It is undrinkable," Mélac says. *Piquette,* or plonk.

He has plenty of drinkable wines among the hanging hams and huge cheeses of his café, a nice Lirac Mélac of his own production from the Gard, for example. But the event of the year is the Château Mélac harvest, held in mid-September to the accompaniment of music and red-robed members of whatever wine confrerie is willing to attend and be photographed.

The grapes are snipped from the drainpipe by anyone with a head for heights and are trampled by young women in vats placed in the street outside the café, after which Mélac pours the brew into bottles where they stay until the filtering at the end of this month. At each harvest the previous year's wine is sold by lottery with the profits going to the local *mairie* to help the quarter's aged. This year, Mélac raised 4,420 francs (about $770).

Production, good year or bad, is always about thirty-five bottles and while his Bastille red might arguably improve if it were aged in barrels instead of the fridge, there isn't enough to fill a barrel. Anyway, the point of the exercise is not to produce a *grand cru* but to get Parisians to grow grapevines. To this end, Mélac recently formed a group called the Vignerons de Paris, a sort of cooperative of urban winegrowers.

According to historians, in the fourth century central Paris was one of the four great French wine-producing regions. Over the centuries, such blights as urban development and phylloxera killed the vineyards with the exception of a small terrain, over-publicized and overpriced, in Montmartre. The *pompiers,* or fire-men, of the ninth arrondissement also produce a small harvest each year and Mélac sees no reason why the practice shouldn't spread.

"Look at the maps, Paris is on just the right latitude," he claims. "There used to be vines on the rue de Charonne, near here. There is the rue des Vignes in Passy—it must have been called that for a reason—and in the twentieth arrondissement you have the rue des Vignoles."

Mélac's Vignerons de Paris is just beginning but he foresees a rosy future with Métro-style maps that will illuminate to point out vineyards around the capital. Each year the urban *vignerons* will bring their grapes to their local *mairies* where they will be weighed by a *huissier*—no serious French function is complete without this august presence—and mixed to form a single brew.

"We'll give the growers back half the wine and the rest will be given to the mayor of Paris and sold for charity. We did it a bit to make fun of all the winemakers' associations. I've been to the Chevaliers de Tastevin, you have to wear a *smoking* or long dress. Why? They overdo. We can do something pleasant and amus-ing—the wines of Paris courtyards."

A country boy from the Aveyron, Mélac took over his father's Paris café in 1978. (His father died the most enviable of deaths, he says, having fallen on his head while fetching a Chablis '69 from his cellar for his wife.) Rather than put up a new shop front sign, he planted his vine, which took at once. One can grow a vine in any part of Paris, he says: He gave a cutting to neighbors to plant in a courtyard otherwise distinguished by cat urine and bi-cycles, and the other day near a Chinese restaurant off the Place de l'Alma he saw a fine vine growing two stories high. "I thought that was terrific," he said.

Mélac puts his Château Mélac into Bordeaux-style bottles because he thinks the labels look better. He expects his Paris *vignerons* to be full of enthusiasm, if not illusions. "It is all symbolic," he said. "After all, if you grow tomatoes on your balcony, they won't be as good as the tomatoes from your grocer but they are your tomatoes."

If plonk de Paris cannot be drunk, can it be used to clean windows or polish cars, at least? No, says Mélac, hurt. It should be put on your chimneypiece, like a painting. "Anyway, it isn't that you really can't drink it. I have. It's just not very good. Sour."

And if one insisted on drinking it, what food would one serve to accompany it? "My God, no one's ever asked me that." He sank into a long silence before coming up with a reply. "A Paris pigeon," he said.

October 30, 1989

ANIMATING PARIS,
CITY HALL STYLE

PARIS—Quite likely Paris was the first city to have street people: the vagabonds or *clochards*. But as in so many other things, Paris is now far behind. Cops keep the *clochards* on the move, the better subway buskers are foreign, the gastronomic pushcarts of New York have yet to be seen, though how nice it would be in Paris to have ambulatory oysters, quiches and crepes.

The mayor of Paris, possibly as bored as everyone else, has decreed that the city's streets be animated. And so any public area these days is likely to be filled with humorless clowns, arthritic acrobats or white-faced mimes, urgently, and not very convincingly, climbing imaginary ropes.

Anyone who thinks that animation can occur by decree would also believe that such animation should be carefully controlled. So the street people, such as they are, are carefully watched by

Paris cops and their moments of spontaneity regulated by the clock.

This summer there were small squeals about liberty of expression when the street performers outside the Pompidou Center on the Beaubourg plateau were told to shut up by 7 P.M. John Guez, who plays the musical saw and does an audience participation version of Three Little Pigs, collected thirty-eight police summonses and a lot of publicity during this summer's silly season when he defended the street entertainers against official repression. "I have nothing against cops," he told a TV crew, "but why bother a clown?"

A reasonable question, but in fact the quality of the animation around Beaubourg has deteriorated badly, and many of the fire-eaters, chain-breakers, storytellers and other so-called entertainers display a lack of talent and an aggressivity that have destroyed the center's earlier *bon enfant* atmosphere. A professional *bon enfant,* sixty-eight-year-old André Dupont, better known as Mouna, says it has changed a lot.

"The atmosphere is different. Everyone is grabbing for the best space. I suggested to the other entertainers that we rotate places and they called me a functionary."

Another regular says the plaza in front of Beaubourg is now just a tacky circus. "People came at first because they were attracted by the colors of the building's pipes, then they found themselves talking to each other. Now no one talks, they're scared to—they think they'll be accused of soliciting or selling drugs. There's no contact, just a lot of passing the hat. The entertainers are businessmen, vulgar, drunk, aggressive."

"You get a better class of people in the Luxembourg Gardens," Mouna says. "I'm turning it into another Speaker's Corner, like Hyde Park."

Mouna, who calls himself an acrobat of ideas, has been haranguing crowds since he abruptly exchanged the restaurant business for the street at the age of forty. "There was a funeral parlor across the street and I started thinking about death and how my life was floating away in bowls of fish soup."

The last true eccentric in the Paris streets, Mouna is a spiritual descendant of the earlier Latin Quarter *farceur* Ferdinand Lops, who proposed that the boulevard Saint Michel be extended to the sea so that students might bathe more often. These days Mouna finds the Sorbonne rather dull and so commutes on his rickety bicycle each day from Montmartre, where he lives, to Beaubourg.

Mouna wears a tape measure around his neck as well as a handy chain of safety pins and carries a variety of accessories from a small new broom (presumably to sweep clean) to a battered red toy telephone, over which he exchanges imaginary conversations with world figures. Over the years he has campaigned for everything from nuclear disarmament to aid for Chilean refugees and is now gathering signatures for a petition against child labor in the Third World.

He has run, unnoticeably, for parliament several times and has also had his knocks from the police. Once he was stopped for leading a procession in which everyone was simply chanting, "We are happy, we are very happy." But by now he is so well established a figure that his presence is almost a sign of respectability in any public place.

Mouna is aware of this. Asked if he intended to cross the few hundred feet that separate Beaubourg from the new Forum des Halles, he replied, "I'm not sure but I think not. Why should I be a walking advertisement for them?"

The new forum, which opened with enormous hype this week, is the first construction, apart from an express subway, to be completed in the disemboweled Halles de Paris. Replanning the Halles has been a subject of discussion for nearly twenty years, and for the last decade the area has been marked by a huge crater, spectacular wheeling and dealing and obscure political maneuvers.

Opening the forum with so much fanfare is the real estate

equivalent of an elephant giving birth to a mouse, for the forum is nothing more than a $153 million underground shopping center.

Not that it is referred to as a shopping center. At the press preview the forum's promoter reiterated that it was to be considered a quarter of Paris, like Saint-Germain-des Prés or Montmartre or, for that matter, Les Halles.

For the opening there was of course a good deal of unspontaneous animation in the streets: a silent merry-go-round, a calliope playing the Merry Widow waltz with dolorous zest and, most astonishingly, an antiseptic version of Mouna.

This elderly man, dressed with embarrassingly careful eccentricity and ajangle with metal accessories pinned to his middle, wore a black bowler and had a neat goatee instead of Mouna's straggly beard. Like Mouna he gives commentaries on contemporary life but they are, alas, couched in classic alexandrine verse.

As an example of the mayor of Paris's sought-for animation, it's a pretty pitiful sight. One longs for Marguerite, the trained bear of the Buci market, or the gorgeously bedizened *clocharde* Simone, now evicted from the Place Dauphine, or even for the men who used to sell neckties out of open umbrellas near the Madeleine. In a word, as an earnest autumn succeeds a dull summer: bring on the clowns.

September 7, 1979

COOKING CLASSES
BY PRINCESS AND COUNTESS

PARIS—The Countess de Mohl telephoned the other day to say that her friend, Princess Marie-Blanche de Broglie, wants to be a very modern princess and that both ladies would like to move out of their circle and meet people who aren't princesses.

Well, it's nice to be able to report that the countess and the princess have indeed found a way to make their dream come true. Over orange drinks served in glasses bearing a gold coronet in the countess's apartment in the sixteenth arrondissement of Paris, the ladies described their plan.

The idea, ultimately, is to found a women's club along the democratic lines of New York's Colony Club, but as this takes time they are easing into things with cooking lessons that the princess will give in her house on the avenue de la Motte-Picquet starting Monday. A demonstration lesson costs 110 francs, food included, and after roll call students and countess and princess alike will eventually tuck into, for example, cheese soufflé, pork chops charcutière and apple tart.

The countess, fine-boned, brunette and charming, and the princess, rounder, blonde and charming, have named their venture Princess Ere 2001.

Princess spelled in the English style without the final "e" may sound *très snob* in France, but it's not intended to.

"It doesn't sound so much like a title," the countess explains.

"More like a joke," the princess suggests.

The 2001 part of the name shows just how farsighted the ladies are. "Everything is called 2000 these days, we want to be ahead," says the countess.

But will there be princesses in the year 2001? "There always have been princesses and there always will be," says the princess, "though not necessarily the same ones."

"The aristocracy has always known how to find new blood," the countess points out.

The princess is an alumna of the Cordon Bleu and a member of the redoubtable ladies' gastronomic society, Les Gourmettes. "Julia Child said I should go into the cooking business," she says. One of her family favorites is called *oeufs tout Paris*.

The countess, on the other hand, says she cannot cook. "In my house they're rather surprised at this project because cooking is not my specialty," she says. But the princess has taught her a dish or two.

"I learned to make roast pork with cloves and pineapple. It had a ravishing name," says the countess.

"*Porc des Iles,*" says the princess.

"And a *bavaroise aux marrons,*" says the countess.

"Nesselrode," explains the princess.

Still, the countess will act mostly as a critic. "I taste and criticize," she says. And the ladies will share bookkeeping duties.

"For me being a princess is a job," says the princess. For the countess, Princess Ere 2001 is the start of a hobby.

"My husband is always off shooting animals and I got tired of standing in fields watching birds drop," she says. "I thought it would be amusing to do something."

The count, sad to say, is not amused by Princess Ere 2001. The prince, who is in computers, is enthusiastic. His family, which is enormously distinguished, has, says the princess, always known how to adapt. Their motto is *"Pour l'avenir."* The countess doesn't know the count's motto but her Baltic baron ancestors bore an equally energetic device: "I carry the lance."

Forging ahead outside their own circle is especially exciting to the countess. "We want to meet people in all milieus. Look at our President. It amuses him to have breakfast with garbage collectors and to visit people impromptu."

"In the past one used one tone of voice to some people, another to others. Paternalism is over," says the countess. "Times are changing."

"Times have changed. In other times a princess wouldn't be cooking," says the princess.

There are projects to visit friends' chateaux and even foreign lands. Although their idea of founding a women's club is heretical in France, the ladies are undaunted.

"One must live in one's epoch," declares the countess.

"Things must start moving," declares the princess.

"The idea is in the air," they declare together.

Television reporters have already been to see the ladies, and while neither they nor their circle saw the program, which was broadcast last Sunday lunchtime, the princess was promptly contacted by a Swiss journalist and a Moroccan restaurateur, and the countess was complimented by her butcher.

Princess Ere 2001 is open to everyone who is talented and interested regardless of class, say the countess and the princess. One feels awful suggesting such a thing in the face of such idealism, but isn't it possible that some social climber might take advantage of the opportunity to break bread with the *gratin,* or upper crust?

"If they wish to improve their position, that shows they've already gone one step higher," says the countess kindly.

"As long as they take that one step with us," the princess says.

January 25, 1975

POTATO OF SNOBS, DAINTY
AND NEWLY CHIC, CAPTIVATES PARIS

PARIS—At this crucial moment the fashions for the coming season in Paris are being determined and with luck we shall never see again the extremes of 1986, when everyone was wearing bubble skirts and drinking a vile blue cocktail based on an excess of curaçao.

Today's fashions, more earthy, seem to require wearing a Saint Laurent–style bunch of grapes at the shoulder and eating *la ratte*. *La ratte* is not at all what you might think. It is a potato. Only in France can a potato be à la mode and have its own public relations consultant.

"We always present it as the queen of potatoes, *la pomme de terre snob*," says the PR woman, Catherine Dufay. *La ratte* is just coming into stores now and will be at its best through mid-March, after which no one gives a fig for potatoes anyway. "I often introduce journalists to *la ratte*," its PR woman says, "and they are delighted."

The first journalist to be delighted was from *l'Express: la ratte,* she noted, was to be found at only the most refined tables. In another magazine *la ratte* was pronounced divine. *Le Monde's* sturdy La Reynière, while deploring the snobbery surrounding the spud, proclaimed his joy at finding it back on the market and declared that it is indeed *la reine des pommes de terre.*

Like so many fashions, *la ratte* is a revival. It was grown in small quantities mostly around Lyon, and was known by such names as the *quenelle de Lyon* and the early pickle, or *cornichon hâtive.* It appears under its present name for the first time in the Vilmorin-Andrieu seed catalogue for 1880.

After World War I, *la ratte* disappeared and it does not even figure in *La Pomme de Terre dans Votre Assiette,* an authoritative guide by Nestor de la Bouteillère, the author of five other books on the subject, including a World War II work called *The Potato as a Source of Fuel.*

The great French potatoes, says de la Bouteillère, are the Belle de Fontenay, the BF-15, the Bintje, the Esterling, the Ker Pondy, the Saucisse and the Rosa. Although there are 1,200 sorts of potatoes, he notes, only 43 are known in France.

The potato came late to France, aided by public relations and fashion. Its great promoter was Antoine Auguste Parmentier, a military pharmacist who urged that potatoes be eaten during the famine of 1770. Parmentier also made the potato à la mode by giving blossoms to Louis XVI, who wore them in his buttonhole. (Marie Antoinette twined hers in her hair.)

Some twenty years after Nestor de la Bouteillère failed to mention *la ratte,* Martine Jolly, in a book called *Merci Monsier Parmentier* (1985), described it as "an exquisite potato, a queen endowed with all the virtues." The book came out just as the chef Joël Robuchon was making Parisians' tongues wag and palates salivate with his remarkable revisionist version of mashed potatoes.

According to *la ratte's* press agent, Robuchon has declared it the champion potato and at a tasting awarded it a record four stars. He is said to use the *ratte* exclusively for his sublime *purée de pommes de terre,* although his 1986 cookbook called for a kilo of BF-15. (The BF-15 potato does not have a public relations rep.)

The revival of *la ratte* began slowly in 1962 when a farmer near Le Touquet, in the north of France, found that the potato flourished in his sandy soil. He began research to improve breeding and emerged with a specimen fine enough to attract the backing of a large cereal producer, the Société Ringot, in 1977. Today, under the leadership of a farmer named Dominique Dequidt, six growers have formed a group devoted to the *ratte,* meeting for tastings every four or five days and exchanging confidences on the blights to which this remarkable root is a prey.

La ratte is no ordinary potato: dainty and small, it should be harvested manually and the growers are fiends for quality control and size.

"People buying *la ratte* expect top quality, it is like going to the haute couture," the PR lady says.

La Ratte du Touquet is marketed in pretty little string bags containing a kilo. Each kilo sells for between ten and thirteen francs, three times the price of some breeds, but *la pomme de terre snob* is no common or garden potato.

"When you have dinner guests you bring out an exceptional wine," Dominique Dequidt says. "Your potatoes, too, should be out of the ordinary."

La Ratte du Touquet can be cooked without being peeled and is said to have a slight hazelnut taste and all possible virtues. The great chefs of France are at this moment turning out recipes, at a fee of thirty thousand francs each, to help launch the potato. The current trend is to invent ways of using it in desserts.

There is only one way in which *la pomme de terre snob* cannot be cooked: it cannot be used for making the popular french fry.

As for its awful, if historic, name, there's nothing much to do about that, and probably early pickle is no more attractive. By insisting on the copyrighted name, La Ratte du Touquet, the growers and their PR lady have done the next best thing and given the potato an aristocratic "*de*" to confirm its inherent fine breeding.

On a more homely level, Mr. Dequidt says that once saturation point has been reached with La Ratte du Touquet (production now is about 1,500 tons a year on sixty hectares of land), his group of growers has another potato they might launch. It is called the *charlotte,* is cheaper, firmly fleshed, and less outstanding in quality.

Unlike La Ratte du Touquet, which is destined for what the French call *le happy few,* Mr. Dequidt says the *charlotte* is perfect for mass consumption.

So the difference between the *charlotte* and the *ratte* is like the difference between the prêt-à-porter and the haute couture?

"Exactly," Mr. Dequidt said.

October 10, 1988

DANIEL COHN-BENDIT:
TEN YEARS AFTER THE EVENTS OF MAY

FRANKFURT—Soon it will be ten years since France exploded with what are still called *les événements,* or the events, a suitably vague term for a moment when poetry was in the streets and panic and hope were in the air. Those who were scared are still not reassured, those who hoped are disappointed: In all, the events and their bright and mischievous student leader, Daniel Cohn-Bendit, are something the French don't really want to talk about.

But despite the silence, memory speaks. No matter which side of the barricade people were on, recent books, articles and exhibitions show a great deal of nostalgia for May 1968.

Daniel Cohn-Bendit, who has lived in Frankfurt since being ejected from France during the events, understands this nostalgia very well. "It was a completely new experience," he says, "when ordinary people felt they were making history." He feels rather nostalgic himself:

"Not that I want to start it up again, but to be in a movement that is a motor of history. . . . " Despite his spunk and cheek, during the events he was often scared; he was also exhilarated when he saw "that our movement represented the collective subjectivity of many people, that what we expressed was an expression of the moment."

May resulted in the retirement of President Charles de Gaulle. To Cohn-Bendit, toppling de Gaulle was not the important thing: "It isn't important that the government fell, but that the way of looking at things changed. Today, everyone, even the President, admits that change is necessary."

"The Lip factory takeover, the women's movement, the concern with immigrants, ecology—all that grew out of May." But these movements are hardly exclusively French. "True, but in France May was the expression of society in movement."

If May was exciting, June 1968 was rough. "It's always depressing to see the end of a movement, even if it's a momentary end." In May Cohn-Bendit had discovered he could manipulate crowds ("I hate chiefs but delighted in being one") and make fools of his distinguished elders. He was interviewed by the media and by Jean-Paul Sartre. He could easily have gone on to star on the international revolutionary circuit. Instead he has deliberately faded into the plodding 1970s, which he regards as a period of transition. His physical appearance—his famous red hair now in lank curls, his plump cheeks unshaven, his shirttails hanging under his out-at-the-elbows sweater—is perhaps the only sign of provocation in a middle-class Frankfurt tearoom where the other young people are dressed as if in an MGM campus musical.

For two years he taught in a Frankfurt kindergarten, work for which his spontaneity and imagination ideally suited him but which he gave up because "after two years no one should teach in a kindergarten, you become mechanical." He worked last month in a leftist bookshop and is now on the dole. He also writes for an underground newspaper whose title, *Pflasterstrand,* recalls the 1968 graffito *Dessous les pavés c'est la plage* (Beneath the cobblestones, the beach), and has fought to help immigrant factory workers. He is, he says with a grin, under the usual amount of police surveillance.

In 1968 Cohn-Bendit was, as he still is, strongly against violence and demagoguery. His most effective tool was humor: "Something revolutionary movements don't know very well," he says, "is how to use ridicule as an arm against absurdity." Maurice Grimaud, who was Paris's prefect of police in 1968, has contrasted Cohn-Bendit's sense of responsibility with the moral collapse of the government and has argued against his expulsion from France. "He was born in the same town as my wife, he's as French as she is," Grimaud says.

This isn't quite true, but Cohn-Bendit's legal situation is curious indeed. Born on April 4, 1945, in Montauban, France, of German parents who had fled Hitler in 1933, Cohn-Bendit went to Frankfurt with his mother in 1958 to join his father, who died the following year. His mother died in 1963, and in 1965 Cohn-Bendit returned to France, where he remained until declared undesirable in 1968.

The law at that time would have given Cohn-Bendit French nationality had he been a resident of France from the age of sixteen to twenty-one. His brother, who is nine years older, is French.

Cohn-Bendit's 1968 expulsion resulted in the extraordinarily moving demonstration in which thousands cried, *Nous sommes tous des juifs allemands* (We are all German Jews). He has made several illegal visits to France since and intends to pop in to fete the tenth anniversary of May.

Daniel Cohn-Bendit is the only person expelled during May 1968 whose expulsion order has not been lifted. A request for an explanation at the Ministry of the Interior leads to a denial that a demand to lift the ban has been made, then to a statement about danger to public order. An attempt to fight through the courts has been unsuccessful: Offered a job by the Paris publisher Belfond, Cohn-Bendit applied to a French administrative court for permission to work in France as a citizen of a Common Market country. The court declared itself incompetent to rule and referred the case to the Common Market court in Strasbourg.

"They just don't want me," Cohn-Bendit says. "It's not a fear that I'll change anything. But a lot of politicians were marked by May in the sense that they were made ridiculous, and they can't forget that.

"Another reason is that traditional politicians have a concept of history that is tied to individuals. May 1968 to them is a person, not a social movement.

"A third reason is that the French police asked the Germans to send my dossier. The dossier showed I haven't changed."

Cohn-Bendit does not believe in a sudden seizure of power but in the gradual disintegration of old values. He says he never felt May would change things overnight: "The paranoid middle classes and de Gaulle, the military man, were terrified because they had no foresight: They expected everything, even if everything was impossible."

He belongs to no political party and describes himself as anti-nuclear, anti-terrorist, an ecologist and a radical critic of society. His talent, he says, is spontaneity and a gift for repartee, neither of which work as well in Germany as in France: "In Germany I was the joker in academic debates," he says of his first years here.

A symbol of failed hopes to some, of potential disorder to others, disliked equally by the Establishment and the far left (in France, he once astutely observed, one has the feeling that no one on the extreme left has children), Daniel Cohn-Bendit may seem to be living in a no-man's-land. This he denies. He has learned a great deal, he says. People may only think of him in terms of May 1968, but, he says, "I don't always compare everything to May."

Indeed, how could he? As he wrote in his book, *Le Grand Bazar,* "In May, 1968, we were realists: We demanded the impossible. Today we don't even dare to face the possible."

April 15, 1978

After serving as deputy mayor in charge of multiculturalism in Frankfurt, Cohn-Bendit was elected as a German member of the European parliament, representing the Green party. He has been awarded honorary degrees, chairs a literary program on Swiss television and told French television on the thirtieth anniversary of May 1968, "These days people like me are thought important for making things move, which I find both funny and, for my own ego, not at all unpleasant." Shortly after, in Paris, he announced that he would run for the European parliament as a French Green, and in June 1999 was triumphantly elected.

HAPPY MEMORIES OF GRAY PARIS
IN THE FIFTIES

PARIS—The city of Paris has the pleasant custom of occasionally putting on exhibitions devoted to the ordinary life of its inhabitants, purposely modest shows recording the memories of an epoch.

The present show, at 29 rue de Rivoli, "C'était Paris dans les Années 50," tells about life in the 1950s, and is, says its curator, Marie-Hélène Parinaud, the first one that is interactive. She uses the word not in its high-tech sense but simply to indicate that thousands of members of the public participated by lending all the objects and photographs on view. Nothing is of value, except to its lenders, and the fact that the show is so humble lends an air of reality.

It also makes such a show harder to put on than one with grander aspirations. "I'd have no problem borrowing a Dior dress," Parinaud says. "I'd get it in five minutes. But to find a blouse made by a neighborhood dressmaker is a lot harder, it's a miracle."

Luckily, Parisians seem to have kept such relics as ration tickets, cheese boxes, bobby pins, toys, newspapers, old banknotes, pre-transistor radios in fake wood and little veiled hats made not by famous milliners but by small *modistes* or by the wearers themselves. As a complement there is a catalogue of collected memories, most of them from ordinary citizens.

The show opens with a dummy wearing a policeman's uniform of the time—round képi and heavy cloak (though not as heavy as it should be since they had weights sewn in the hem so they could be swung as a weapon during riots). It begins with the war's end in 1945 and ends in 1959. The period covered is one of poverty and hope.

It was a time when ordinary people had iceboxes and not refrigerators, and blocks of ice were still delivered by horse-drawn wagons, when there were first-run and neighborhood movie houses, not multiplexes, when the sign *Eau à tous les étages* meant that many apartments had no running water of their own. Schoolchildren wore dark smocks and teachers thought theirs was the finest profession in the world. Streets were empty enough to play in, buses had open platforms at the back, lottery tickets were sold from outdoor booths, the métro had wooden seats and tickets were punched by uniformed attendants.

Prisoners of war and deportees were delivered to the Gare du Nord or the Gare de l'Est and deposited at the Hotel Lutétia for processing. Food was scarce and the bread, says one witness, was yellow and heavy because the minister in charge spoke British, and not American, English and asked the Americans for "corn," the British word for wheat. The black market thrived but is hardly mentioned, although one witness says it was particularly active for false teeth.

Coal was rationed and one witness recalls that during the icy winter of 1945–46, his father would go to the boulevard des Batignolles, which was still covered in tar-coated wooden cobblestones, to pinch firewood.

Streets echoed with the cries of knife grinders, window-pane installers, food vendors, the noise of metal garbage bins being collected and street singers. If Bandit and Sortilège were coveted perfumes, the streets smelled more of unwashed Parisians (street sweepers were allowed one shower a week) and the metal outdoor toilets called *vespasiennes*.

It was a time of privation and great joy and discovery—of jazz and blue jeans, nylon stockings and parachutes (excellent for wedding dresses) and of the GIs who brought them. The theme of the show is recovered pleasures in a very gray Paris whose façades had not yet been cleaned under order of de Gaulle's minister of culture, André Malraux.

Paris was divided into villages, each with its own atmosphere, and people went out as much as possible to escape their overcrowded flats (many would hock their winter clothes in summer and vice versa, using the municipal pawnshop as a huge closet). Everything was on a smaller scale. One witness recalls a grocery store-café, on the Place Dauphine, so tiny that the regulation sign about public drunkenness, *Loi sur la répression de l'ivresse publique,* had to be glued on the ceiling.

The show has record jackets and posters for new stars such as Yves Montand or the Compagnons de la Chanson and for the operettas in which the emollient Luis Mariano gleamed. There was a Luna Park at the Porte Maillot and the six-day bicycle races at the velodrome d'hiver.

The model living rooms and kitchens show spindly legged furniture covered in synthetic materials, Formica in the kitchens and, as a sign of new prosperity, a primitive washing machine and a bulbous Frigidaire. There is also a 4CV Renault: waiting lists for new cars could last for years, and two of the most popular annual exhibitions were the Automobile Show and the Salon des Arts

Ménagers (household equipment exhibition), both held at the prestigious Grand Palais.

By 1954 Abbé Pierre had founded his mission to help the poor, in its way a sign of growing prosperity because earlier people would have had nothing to donate. The same year automobile horns were banned and parking tickets began to be issued. Also in 1954, there was a Vespa rally, the nicely designed motorized bicycle having had a huge success, especially among the young, and Citroën introduced a luxury sedan, the DS, sleekly modern but delivered with a crank just in case.

The first Club Méditerranée opened in 1950, although no one mentions it, but a suggestion of brighter, and looser, times ahead comes with the popularity of gingham dresses introduced by Brigitte Bardot in *Et Dieu Créa la Femme*.

The show gives a feeling of a happy and hopeful time, which is clearly how those who lived it want to remember it. No one mentions the Marshall Plan, the Cold War, the loss of Indochina, the start of the Algerian war. Parinaud says that the witnesses she spoke to didn't remember who the president of the republic was at the time, or speak of the strikes or of the regiments that were going off to fight. "No, no, not a word," she says.

"Contrary to what people say, it wasn't all as rose-colored as that," she says. "People beautify things—it was past and so it was good."

Of today's French population, 67 percent had not been born in 1950. For the others, as the show suggests, nostalgia is all that it used to be, and then some.

May 3, 1997

VIONNET,
LAST OF THE GREAT COUTURIERS

PARIS—Madeleine Vionnet, the last of the great couturiers and possibly the greatest one of all, died quietly in her house in Auteuil on Sunday. "No one," Christian Dior once wrote, "has ever carried the art of dressmaking further than Vionnet." She would have been ninety-nine years old in June.

Although she closed down her house thirty-five years ago and was a quiet, down-to-earth workhorse in the peacock world of fashion, Vionnet has remained a key name to anyone interested in fashion history, and in recent years she has also been discovered by the young, thanks largely to Cecil Beaton's twentieth-century fashion show at the Victoria and Albert in 1971, and to the recent exhibition at New York's Metropolitan Museum, where, as one critic put it, she stole the show.

As Beaton points out, Vionnet's genius lay in her use of materials. She invented the bias cut—the equivalent, in fashion, of having invented the wheel—and so, as Beaton says, with her scissors she changed fashion.

Her discovery, which did away with tricky fastenings and hard seams, allowing fabric to fall with a new naturalness, was all the more extraordinary for someone born early in the last quarter of the nineteenth century whose first important job was with the fine but fusty house of Callot Soeurs. After Callot she worked for the well-established house of Doucet, where vendeuses would push her models aside when clients came, and where she invented the bias cut. "I wanted it and found it," she would later say of this historic moment. "It seemed natural."

She gave clothes a new suppleness. "I liked supple fabrics—crepes," she said a few years ago. "I work in others, of course, but that's what I like." She was never able to use the past tense for very long when talking about work.

Madeleine Vionnet was born in a very modest family from the Jura Mountains of France, where she will be buried this week. Her parents wanted her to be a teacher so she could support herself, but a dressmaker friend pointed out that, even with scholarships, her family would be stuck with her clothing bills until she was twenty-five. So, at eleven, Madeleine became a dressmaker's apprentice. Before working for Callot and Doucet, she worked for Kate Reilly in London. She opened her house, then located on the rue de Rivoli, in 1912.

Plump in her years of triumph, she was tiny and unflagging in old age, with astonishingly vivid dark eyes. "Look at this, I love it," she once said, pulling out a drawing of herself at the age of one. Except for her eyes, she was one small blur. "Look at those eyes," she would laugh.

Even when she had become Paris's top fashion figure, Vionnet was happiest in the ateliers with her fellow craftsmen. The American photographer Thérèse Bonney, who first went to the house of Vionnet in 1921, says one never saw Vionnet at parties. She wore severely tailored suits and a little top hat, had no sense of publicity or salesmanship (her vendeuses often had to ask her to go away because she tended to ruin sales). She was a worker, not a personality.

Her showrooms on the avenue Montaigne were a model of restrained elegance, with glass by Lalique, Japanese prints and modern rugs. Her clothes were shown without hats or accessories on very tall, impolite models.

Vionnet was the first to discover the wealthy South Americans who are still the mainstay of couture. She invented a way to foil copyists by putting her thumbprint on the label of each dress. She was the first to install a canteen for her workers—who at one point numbered a thousand—and she gave paid vacations before the law required it.

She created her designs by draping fabrics over a small wooden dummy. She was against sketching: "People who draw don't have a sense of material," she would say, "though perhaps they have more sense of color and fantasy."

She hated anything showy, costumish or faddy. "Softness," she said, "is always good."

She never missed a Balenciaga collection, despite her great age, and he made clothes for her, free, of course. The last thing he made for Vionnet before he closed his house in 1968 was a pair of print hostess pajamas with a long coat.

Vionnet also had her dislikes. Chanel, she said shortly, was a good businesswoman. Schiaparelli was "not a couturier." Poiret? "No, no, no! But he had good artists working for him."

Her Auteuil town house was all discreet beiges, with parchment-covered walls, sharp-angled furniture and an imposing portrait of herself in lacquer and eggshell by Jean Dunand.

In her later years she read a great deal in French and English and also owned several books in Russian (she had been briefly married to a Russian). "I don't speak Russian, though I learned to read it and translate it, which isn't bad," she said.

It was illuminating and exalting to hear her talk about her work, but she had shrewd insights on many subjects. "Almost always when you see a painting called 'Mother of the Painter' it is good," she once said. Or, going through a book on the history of costume, she might explain why mutton-chop sleeves were ugly and hoop skirts nice.

Vionnet was aware of her place in history, and if she was rightly pleased by the renewed interest in her work, she also knew this showed the bankruptcy of current fashion. "One must evolve, not revive," she would say.

Once, during a conversation, she suddenly said, "Do you write about the couture?" No. "That's good," she said, "because it doesn't exist anymore."

March 4, 1975

THE FINE ART
OF WINDOW SHOPPING

PARIS—The genius of French stores has always been measured profusion: Ali Baba reviewed by Descartes. The recent trend is to call in well-known architects to design shops, and their quests for the pure and immaterial are not always in accord with the shopper's perhaps impure but pleasant dreams of material acquisition. Present-day minimalist shop design can be so bare and stark that the decor almost says caveat emptor: there is less here than meets the eye.

A show at the Pavillon de l'Arsenal, which specializes in Paris architecture and urban planning, is called Vitrines d'Architecture: Les Boutiques à Paris (Showcases of Architecture: Paris Shops). It traces the history of Paris shops and above all celebrates the contemporary architect's hand in colored photographs mounted on severe plate glass. It is clearly an architect's, rather than a shopper's, show.

In early times, shops were around the Ile de la Cité, which was then a part of the port leading from the Mediterranean to Flanders, and the shops were on bridges. Most of the business was conducted on the street, the shop itself more of a storehouse with some goods displayed on shutters that folded down into makeshift tables. Shop windows did not appear until the end of the seventeenth century.

In the late eighteenth century the city's first purpose-built shopping center was created by the duc d'Orléans at the Palais-Royal, causing Louis XVI to remark, "Cousin, now that you are a shopkeeper I suppose we'll only see you on Sundays." The duke's little fling in real estate soon gave rise to one of the glories of French shopping, the glass-covered passages that appeared in the early nineteenth century's building boom.

Covered passages lined with shops were not a French invention (and fewer than half of those built in Paris still exist), but they were typically Parisian in their zestful commercialism. They have been called the precursor of the shopping mall, which is true in the sense that a *tournedos Rossini* is a precursor of the Big Mac. The passages offered relief from filthy, ill-drained streets (Paris had no sidewalks until 1826), and strollers could window-shop— goods were for the first time displayed in shop windows—and stroll in seductive gas light, introduced in 1816 in the Passage Montesquieu.

The shopkeepers' status had changed: they were now retailers selling cleverly displayed luxury and novelty goods. The *passages couverts* were alluring, sexy even as rendezvous spots, still interesting enough in our century to win the attention of Walter Benjamin and the surrealists. They were also an intermediate step to the department store.

Department stores existed before Baron Haussmann remodeled Paris, but they burgeoned in the mid-nineteenth century,

minimal displays

rich temples of plenty, models of the engineer's skilled use of metal and concrete that reached its apogee with the Eiffel Tower. They were monuments to exuberant consumerism: "Everywhere space had been gained, air and light entered freely, the public moved about as it wished. . . . It was the cathedral of modern commerce, solid and light, created for the client," Zola wrote in *Au Bonheur des Dames,* said to have been modeled on the Bon Marché, founded in 1869.

A later development was the specialized luxury boutique, and in the 1920s the annual Salon des Artistes Décorateurs featured shops designed by Mallet-Stevens, Chareau and Herbst. Couturiers such as Madeleine Vionnet in her avenue Montaigne shop created a luxurious, comfortable background in which clothes were shown at their leisurely best. A reaction to what Zola had called "the neurosis of big bazaars," modern luxury stores became a symbol of discreet swank. When post–May 1968 "revolutionaries" wanted to protest against modern consumerism, they took Fauchon, the opulent food store, as their Bastille.

The Arsenal's exhibition of contemporary shops is divided into Paris Fashion, Paris Decoration, Paris Culture and Unusual Paris, the last being a grab bag of old and lovable shops such as Dehillerin (kitchen utensils), the Madeleine Gély umbrella shop on the boulevard St. Germain, shoemakers, exterminators, taxidermists and—not at all old but staggering in its savory richness—Tang Brothers, the Chinese supermaket on the avenue d'Ivry. These days only in Paris street markets, food stores and ethnic souks are profusion and its miscellaneous delights still celebrated.

The Paris Culture section includes bookstores, the Virgin Megastore in the 1930s National City Bank building on the Champs Elysées and the boutiques that have become a basic feature in all museums. The museums, with their catalogue sales and franchise operations, may point to the shopping future—the virtual boutique.

In the meantime, many of the new architect-designed boutiques, which are the center of the exhibit, suggest that shopping can become if not virtual at least so savourless that all the sensuous pleasures traditionally involved disappear before an imagined purity that perhaps dissipates guilt but also annihilates fun.

Some of the examples are warm and welcoming but it is clear that the favored tendency is for the shop, like the art gallery, to become, in today's jargon, a space. Abetted by the use of plastic cards, the sense of transaction has been erased: shopping, which is essentially the game between the lure and the allured, has gone lite.

Articles so artfully arranged as to seem untouchable, minimalist decor, consumption at its most invisible and, paradoxically, at its most costly—profusion and its delights are banned.

Not surprisingly, several of the architects interviewed for the show's catalogue single out for acclaim the gelid interior of Jil Sander's shop in Vionnet's former premises on the avenue Montaigne, now the most luxurious shopping street in Paris. It is praised for being "intensely empty" and for "assassinating the bourgeois model of the avenue Montaigne." Bewildering for the bourgeois who is, after all, the customer of the architect-designed boutiques.

Perhaps Christo was a visionary back in 1964 when he designed what he called Storefront No. 4. It is a completely blank façade, both its entrance and shop window covered from top to bottom by a totally bare curtain.

July 19, 1997

SAINT-GERMAIN'S
LATEST BRAINSTORM

PARIS—Saint-Germain-des-Prés, which has long considered itself the most intelligent quarter of Paris, will soon be welcoming a
breed whose only degree is in rapid currency calculation: the international shopper.

The Drugstore Publicis in the heart of St. Germain will, in the
course of this year, become an Emporio Armani, the hairdresser
Claude Maxime just across from Picasso's lovely bust in memory
of Guillaume Apollinaire has shut and will reopen as a Dior men's
store. Opposite the entrance to the church of Saint-Germain-des-
Prés, the ancient jeweler Arthus Bertrand, which specializes in
decorous engagement rings and christening cups, has ceded half
its space to Louis Vuitton where, for 7900 francs, one can buy the
canonical brown and yellow case to put the cups and rings in.

The rumor that Hermès was going to take over the excellent

bookshop, La Hune, just between the Flore and Deux Magots cafés, turned out to be false, but the tempest in the espresso cup has been enough to induce the mayor of the sixth arrondissement, Jean-Pierre Lecoq, to issue a statement saying that he regards the changes in his fief as normal economic evolution. He added that he had asked the minister of culture to classify as inviolable monuments the terraces and façades of the Deux Magots, the Flore and the Brasserie Lipp, "three famed establishments which are part of the mythic character and memory of Saint-Germain-des-Prés."

Presumably if they wished, the three famed establishments could turn their interiors into shoe shops or designer boutiques but they are doing very well on their mythic character already, unlike the neighborhood's nightclubs, which are dying out. Possibly in anticipation of the new shopping clientele, the Flore, which has always been tiresome about credit cards, now welcomes American Express. It has not begun serving caffe latte.

The two cafés and Lipp have been the center of Saint-Germain since the period between the wars, when writers and publishers began meeting there. The atmosphere was stuffily provincial—during a heat wave in July 1922, Louis Aragon was thrown out of the Deux Magots for removing his jacket—and even during the brief wave of jitterbugging bohemians after World War II, Jacques Prévert, living in Montmartre, remarked of Saint-Germain-des-Prés, "It was never a real quarter. It had neither peanut vendors nor whores."

Rather than a quarter, Saint-Germain-des-Prés is usually described as a village, with its rivalries (from the 1930s through World War II Lipp was considered right wing, the Flore left) and piously conserved traditions (Le Petit Saint Benoit claims to be the only restaurant that still has a *casier à serviettes,* wooden pigeonholes for patrons' napkins). The tall Romanesque steeple of Saint-Germain-des-Prés is the village church.

Jean-Paul Sartre lived with his mother above the Deux Magots;

Simone de Beauvoir lived at the nearby Hotel Louisiane and noted that the style for café intellectuals was to "spend the day exhaling disgust in blasé little phrases cut by yawns." This would later becoming an identifying characteristic of existentialism, a word de Beauvoir had never heard when it was first applied to her although she enjoyed the fame it brought. She had become a mainstay of the Flore simply because it had a coal stove to huddle by in the icy days of the Occupation.

By the end of World War II the village was marketing "existentialism" with an expertise today's retailers would envy, a picture of "two dispirited existentialists named Gréco and Vadim" even driving de Gaulle off the front page of *Samedi-Soir* when he announced his new political platform. Sartre, Mauriac and Merleau-Ponty wrote songs for Juliette Gréco, and when the opportunity arose she exchanged her meaningful black clothes for the New Look of Dior.

Today's village intellectuals are as likely to be discussing the merits of pin-wale versus wide-wale corduroy as hermeneutics. Their star is Bernard-Henri Lévy, who hangs out on the first floor of the Flore, formerly a gay stronghold, and is as famous for his plunging neckline as his ideas. The Deux Magots opened a Tokyo branch in 1989 and Franck Daffis of Le Petit Saint Benoit says his famous *hachis parmentier* already figures in Japanese guidebooks. He is ready to welcome shoppers and the ladies who lunch but does not intend to offer them low-calorie salads.

"That," he says severely, "would be the end of the restaurant business."

The beginning of the end, it was wrongly predicted, came in the mid-1960s, when the Drugstore Publicis replaced the dusty old Royal Saint Germain café. No one seems to regard the replacement of the Drugstore by an Emporio Armani as a further sign of decline, Sonia Rykiel already having taken over the beloved restaurant des Saints Pères, and the village having since the 1970s become a center for interior decorators and costly fabric stores. The expansion of Prada on the rue de Grenelle, just behind the boulevard Saint Germain, became proof that the village can be as potent for retailers as the so-called golden triangle on the Right Bank, pure pinchbeck except for its glittering hypotenuse, the avenue Montaigne.

The new shops are less a revolution than a return to things as they were in Saint-Germain-des-Prés. Before it became a café, Les Deux Magots, in 1813, opened as a luxury store. The only difference is that in those days the word was not Emporio but emporium.

January 6, 1996

SIMONE SIGNORET:
A MEMORY

PARIS—When someone treasured dies it is as if time should stop for a moment and life skip a beat. Not life on our great and heedless globe, but at least in the Place Dauphine, the small square in the center of Paris where Simone Signoret and Yves Montand had a ground-floor flat that had a rather English air of coziness and a mirror over the chimneypiece in which she had stuck snapshots of family and friends and the children of friends. Simone loved the small village that is the Place and once gave me a traveling clock that showed time zones all over the world.

"In case," her card said, "you *really* want to know what time it is outside the Place Dauphine."

In recent weeks the brown awnings over the closed windows of her apartment looked so limp that one could only quickly turn away and hope the day had not yet come. When it did come on

Monday, a small group of photographers gathered at her door, probably more from shock than from news sense, for they knew she had died in her country house about an hour's drive from Paris.

Around the photographers people dined in outdoor restaurants and workers played *boules* as if it were just another Indian summer day.

Life went on in part because of the shock and the unexpected sorrow. The French knew they had admired Simone Signoret; they learned that they had also loved her. *Le Monde,* the afternoon of her death, gave her a front-page headline and then said at great length that it was impossible to know what to say about her. In its awkwardness, it was the most heartfelt obituary I have ever read in France.

Before I knew her, I thought of Simone Signoret simply as the finest screen actress since World War II. She was fearless in her range—from the radiant Casque d'Or to the betrayed Alice in *Room at the Top,* to the raddled Madame Rosa—and she was never happier than when working with a film crew. When shooting ended, she always seemed, and said she felt, orphaned.

Orphaned perhaps, but surrounded by friends. She had extraordinary delicacy—the French word *pudeur* says it best—and also she was the best storyteller one could hope to meet; one misses most, I think, the people one has laughed with the most.

One reason she was such a good storyteller was her remarkable memory. Memory was deeply important to her—she saw it as an often inconvenient treasure. "My memories don't belong to me. The moment one is talking about oneself one is talking about others as well," she said.

Her autobiography, *Nostalgia Isn't What It Used to Be,* is in a sense about memory and about her attempts never ever in life to fall for the lure of forgetfulness.

Her last book and first novel was for many months on this year's best-seller lists. It was called *Adieu Volodia* and it was a vast panoramic tale centered on a cast of Jewish immigrants in Paris from early in the century to after World War II. In part it was a call to remember the small vanished craftsmen of Paris, the streets that had been bulldozed, the Jews who had been taken away, though when it came to sending her characters to Nazi death camps Simone, for once in her life, lost courage.

"I came to love those characters. They just came, one by one, and I wasn't expecting them," she said at lunch a few months ago. "I wasn't expecting anything. Finally, I had to end the book because I was in danger of never ending it, I was enjoying it too much, telling myself a story I didn't even know until I had told it."

Instead of sending her Jewish characters to die at the hands of the Nazis, she killed off some of them in a real train crash that made headlines in France in the 1930s. "I couldn't face seeing them deported. It's a gift I wanted to give them, that they would be celebrated and respected in death. Because there was a great difference between the deaths of people who died in that train wreck and the people who disappeared later in the camps."

As it turned out, that was our last lunch in the Place Dauphine. Sometimes we would eat on the sidewalk at Chez Paul, just outside Simone's window so if the telephone rang she could reach inside and answer it. Sometimes we would eat a few yards down the block at the Caveau du Palais. I remember on a bright winter day at the Caveau hearing a noise outside in the Place while we were having another last coffee. The noise came from a straggly group of protesters shouting slogans against Montand. It turned out they were an animal protection group and Montand was a prominent member of an anti-cancer league that possibly countenanced animal experimentation.

Simone listened to the shouting, then ambled to the telephone to call Montand, who was at home, two doors away. "Listen," she said, "there's a bunch of people outside the restaurant demonstrating against you. They seem to have come to the wrong address."

Within seconds, Montand was out of the flat and on the Place and Simone was at his side. I left them talking to the demonstrators.

An hour later, Simone telephoned. She and Montand had invited the protesters into their apartment, she said, and they had a long talk. "I told them they didn't know a thing about demonstrating and I gave them a few pointers," she said. The demonstrators left the apartment, revitalized. "And they ended up loving me," Simone added, laughing, "which was, of course, the point."

October 4, 1985

RITES & RULES

PARIS—LA FRANCE PROFONDE
COMES BACK TO TOWN

PARIS—It was the Americans who naively posed the question, "How're you going to keep them down on the farm after they've seen Paree?" Parisians by tradition hang on to the best of both worlds, city slickers who are hayseeds at heart. No word in the French language is as loved as *le terroir* (the soil), especially by those who do not need to live from it.

Each year, as the newspaper headlines put it, The Country Comes to Paris. The occasion is the international Salon de l'Agriculture, where for one week the huge Porte de Versailles exposition ground becomes one vast farmyard. This year's show was opened by President Jacques Chirac, who spent hours chatting up farmers, poking cattle, and sampling food of the *terroir*. He was followed by every politician who knows which side his baguette is buttered on, French farmers being among the country's most fractious voters.

If it is politically wise to attend the Salon, the interest of most visitors comes straight from the heart. As the writer Alain Schiffres has noted, the Parisian's feeling for the country comes from a sense of confinement and nostalgia: within every Parisian, he says, beats the heart of an Auvergnat.

And so each year the crowds pile in, making recent block-busters like the Cézanne exhibition seem like a flop. There are real farmers in flat caps, windbreakers and home-knit sweaters, large-bellied, red-cheeked and narrow-eyed; there are foreign livestock buyers, but above all there are Parisians eating up the sights and smells—and food—of the *terroir*. Farmworkers prod the exhibits past gaping visitors into the showring and the organiz-ers provide the ambience: plangent hunting horns, a distant cow-bell and even a refuse bin filled with cardboard boxes and plastic bags but evocatively labeled *fumier* (manure).

The real lure is the animals, all looking double life-size when seen close up in their pens, making adult visitors into goggle-eyed children. Can one really tell the difference between a Berrichon de Cher and a Berrichon de l'Indre? Nope, except the Indre sheep has the snooty gaze of a llama. Can one in fact tell the sheep from the goats? Not always. And how to guess that a North of England Mule is, confusingly, a sheep.

The Large White pig fits its name admirably, the Smallest Horse in the World is a quarter the size of a Large White, looks scatty and sells for eighteen thousand francs. The workhorses—the noble Percheron, the German Schwarzwälder Kalt-blutpferd—are wonderful with their short neat bodies, furry an-kles and feet like soup plates. The cows and bulls are mostly asleep, just as well as the Salon is in a sense a memento mori for most of its live exhibits.

Lamb chops and gigots are displayed with startling lack of tact, and near the vaunted Coutancie cattle are cuts of Coutancie steak (like Kobe beef, the Coutancie is said to get its quality from being massaged, and one of the heifers is getting the treatment,

which turns out to be a fluffy red roller, like one in a car wash, rolling over her sleepily contented back).

There is heavy farm machinery, rustic furniture, and near the Solognote sheep there are sweaters and shirts made from their beige wool. One man sits at a Rube Goldberg device with jiggling bobbins, which extrudes hairy socks. Traditionalists can buy Barbour jackets and shotguns and riding kit.

What everyone buys—or, more satisfyingly, samples free of charge—are the products from every inch of the *terroir*. Pâtés, terrines, sausages, country hams, cheeses, rillettes and rillons, as well as soft ice cream from Italy, organic brioches, wines, ciders, rum punches from the overseas territories, and even milk. Ostrich pâté samples were going nicely (there are also four live ostriches shown by an Italian company), and this year for the first time fish are included in the agricultural show, which means plates of oysters and smoked salmon, smoked trout and pink crevettes as well.

The show has plenty of worthy and evitable pedagogical displays and booths offering farmers loans, insurance and job placement advice. There are also seminars on "Corporate Partnerships between the European Union and Central European Countries in the Animal Sector" and on "Examples in Goat Breeding for Improved Performance."

With an annual turnover of 290 billion francs, agricultural products are big business, which is not why Parisians visit the show. They go for the same reason that a prefect of police, Maurice Grimaud, declared the hunting season open in Paris some years back, although hunting is illegal in Paris. He wanted people on their way to work to have the illicit pleasure of imagining that they were walking on leaves instead of asphalt, that instead of exhaust fumes they were breathing the fresh dawn air and that traffic cops were game wardens in disguise. In a word, to dream.

March 2, 1996

MONEY SPEAKS
IN FRANCE

PARIS—The *Wall Street Journal* may be forgiven—although not, apparently, by the French government—for suggesting that France's new anti-inflation plan will, to the contrary, increase the rate of inflation. The *Wall Street Journal* should be forgiven because no economic theory that makes sense elsewhere can be applied to France, where money is a different substance from anywhere else.

The French say Americans are always talking about money. It could with equal truth be said that the French are always thinking about it. The materialism of each country is different. Each French franc, each centime seems to have a palpable existence. In America, money has a more abstract quality: It is thought of in terms of what it will buy. A man will be said in the United States to be worth x amount of dollars; in French one says "his surface" is x amount of francs, a phrase dating back to the days when wealth was measured in acres.

The American phrase "She looks like a million dollars" makes no sense to the French, although they rightly find it repellent. In America, money is something that will grow. In France, it is something to hold on to. Americans want money to move; the French are afraid it will move out of their grasp. Americans invest; the French tuck away. Wars and financial crises have made the ideal French investment a gold bar buried on a piece of one's own land; there have been too many property busts for land in the United States to have the absolute value it has here, and Americans are not salting away gold bars although they do invest in gold-mine shares.

A French money manager, asked if he advised his clients to invest in French equities, replied, "Almost never." Americans boast about their salaries and investments. The Frenchman, remarks a Paris banker, would never boast of having made a killing, for it would let the world know he had money.

There is nothing more private than money. The singer Juliette Gréco was once interviewed at length on her love life. When the interviewer asked how much she earned, she bridled. "Some things," she said, "are private."

In France, the notion of money is invested with the anxiety of impermanence, a fear that it will be taken away. Gertrude Stein wrote, "Anyway the French people never take money very seriously, they save it certainly, they hoard it very carefully but they know really that it has no very great permanence. That is the reason they all want a place in the country."

The French view of money seems even to affect the French seasons. The autumn, a rich and lush time in other places, is crabbed and pinched here because it is tax time and school-fee time and the time when the cost of having lived it up on summer holiday catches up. While in New York and London, September and October mark the crackling start of a new season, here it is known as the *rentrée,* the return from vacation, the return to grim real life, a return made even more numbing this year by Prime Minister Raymond Barre's belt-tightening anti-inflation plan.

The Barre plan and its permutations have made this autumn especially morose and the subject of money even more overbearing than usual. The lively leftist weekly *Le Nouvel Observateur* (from which the above anecdote about Juliette Gréco was taken) has brought a certain freshness to the subject with a three-part series, "La Fortune des Français," directed by staff journalist Josette Alia (salary nine thousand francs per month).

The first issue in the series sold out immediately, for in it the journalists somehow persuaded France's leading political figures, from Gaullist to Communist, to list their assets (or *patrimoine* in French, a much richer-sounding word suggesting the accumulations of the years). As may be expected, the political leaders tumbled all over each other to show how little they possess.

In the second part of the series, the magazine asked, is the French attitude to money different from other people's? Yes.

Quoting an OECD report, the introductory article notes that France is the only country to combine republican egalitarianism with the utter inviolability of the strongbox.

Avarice is found to be peculiarly French and is traced by the sociologist Jean-Paul Aron in *Le Nouvel Observateur* to the revolution, when the peasant, who had been subservient to the landowner and the church, suddenly found himself free but still attached to his ancient reflex of hiding his possessions for fear that his masters might seize them. Even when the peasant became in time a salaried bourgeois, this atavism remained.

"Avarice," Mr. Aron continues, "is the contrary of exchanging and circulating wealth; it is accumulation, pinning down. This avarice is the perfect explanation of an economy that is based on the value of real property, the earth."

The earth, like gold, is infinitely reassuring, according to another contributor to the series, the psychiatrist René Held. A miser, he adds, is still at the anal stage of development and he is likely to suffer from constipation.

Dr. Held's remarks make a rather jarring detail of the Barre anti-inflation plan fall into place. At the same time as major measures, it was announced that the government health service would no longer reimburse citizens for the purchase of laxatives. Why such a detail at such a time, one wondered. Dr. Held's theory makes the reason clear. The government is encouraging avarice, with its attendant constipation, as part of its tightening measures on consumer spending.

The *Wall Street Journal* thinks, of course, that money should be encouraged to circulate freely instead of being blocked up, but then it is not for them or for us to try to change the French. The Barre plan may lead to an explosion or it may be giving the French what they secretly want. To quote again from Gertrude Stein on the French attitude to money:

"Money to spend is not very welcome, if you have it and you try to spend it, well spending money is an anxiety, saving money is a comfort and a pleasure, economy is not a duty it is a comfort, avarice is an excitement, but spending money is nothing, money spent is money nonexistent, money saved is money realized."

October 30, 1976

GETTING THROUGH FRANCE'S
LINGUISTIC JUNGLE

PARIS—Officially, France has since the time of de Gaulle frowned on foreign intrusions into the language, such as *franglais*. This has been interpreted as mindless chauvinism while in fact it is simply an indication that basic French is so complex that its users do not wish to have to cope with imported words as well.

One would think, for example, that after all these centuries the French would have decided which countries have a *"la"* in front of their names and which a *"le."* Not at all: It was only in March that the Quai d'Orsay, working apparently at the same pace as the Académie Française with its dictionary, announced which sex various foreign countries belong to.

Against this sort of local linguistic confusion, what chance has the visitor, however well versed in the imperfect subjunctive or the past definite? The answer is, very little. French is not a language but a state of mind.

One clue to the state of mind is to think negatively. Rather than say outright that the weather is cold or hot, say it is *pas chaud* or *pas froid*. Rather than praise someone as good-looking or attractive, say that he or she is *pas mal*.

In general, beware of the addition of a soothing adjective or adverb. A *petite facture* (small bill) should be more closely scrutinized than a plain *facture*. A *petit moment* is much longer than just a *moment*. So is a *bon moment*. If something is *légèrement en retard* (slightly late) that is much worse than being simply *en retard*. A woman who is in the *soixantaine* is sixtyish, *la bonne soixantaine* adds years. As for *la soixantaine bien sonnée*, time doesn't march on, it lopes.

This brings up the whole question of time, which bewilders any foreigner trying to live in France. French time is not only confusing, it often seems downright malicious.

Most countries have seasons or months. The French year is divided into two periods: *les vacances* (vacation) and *la rentrée* (the return from vacation). Vacation is July and August, followed by the monthlong *rentrée*. The months in between do not count except for *les fêtes du nouvel an* (Christmas) and *vacances scolaires* (school vacations), which are movable feasts scheduled to fall at the time when you most need a plumber.

The shortest period of time in France seems to be *une minute*. An *instant* is longer and a *petit instant* is, of course, longer still. A *petit moment* is worse, somewhat longer than eternity.

A week in France is popularly a *huitaine* (eight days). Two weeks is a *quinzaine* (fifteen days). If someone says he will meet you *vers* (toward) six o'clock, it means after, not going on. If he says *à bientôt*, you may meet in the future. If he says *à très bientôt*, he means he hopes to God he won't see you again but he knows he'll have to.

The French sense of time obeys its own secret logic. As one

exasperated foreigner remarked, "The French are so logical that they don't make sense." Exaggerated perhaps, but the foreigner had probably just been to a dry cleaner who said come back in the course of the *semaine*. That, of course, means next week, not this. Even the foreigner who accepts the ground rules will find that in France time often means *temps perdu*. No point in losing further time in questioning such simple imponderables as why, if a French week has eight days, does the piece of furniture known as a *semainier* have only seven drawers?

April 25, 1986

EXEMPLARY,
BEARDED CLÉMENTINE

PARIS—Mme Clémentine Delait was a devoted wife and mother, plumply attractive in the late-nineteenth-century way, a skilled needlewoman much loved by her fellow citizens of Thaon-les-Vosges. She died thirty years ago this month and has been almost forgotten, which is surprising, for in her day Clémentine Delait was the most illustrious and celebrated bearded lady in France.

A few remember her. Jean Nohain and François Caradec have just written her biography, *The Exemplary Life of the Bearded Lady, Clémentine Delait, 1865–1939,* and Charles Grossier, now ninety, has the fondest memories of her. Mr. Grossier was Mme Delait's barber: "I went to her house three times a week to give her beard a special shampoo," Mr. Grossier told Messrs. Nohain and Caradec. "When I trimmed it, she watched me like a hawk. She took care of that beard, she washed it, she clucked over it,

THAON-les-VOSGES. - Madame Delait

Photo Homeyer et Ehret, Epinal - Reproduction interdite   Exiger le cachet de Mme Delait

Madame Clémentine Delait.
Collection M. A. Maffeis

she brushed it every day. What a charming woman, though when it came to her beard she fussed like a mother hen."

What makes Mme Delait's story so pleasing is her evident joy in being bearded. While today's bearded ladies are probably secretive and neurotic, Mme Delait was complacent and even coquettish about her beard, which, in the fullness of time, surpassed even that of her brother Auguste and brought fame to the Café Delait (later renamed the Café de la Femme à Barbe) in Thaon-les-Vosges, near Epinal.

Clémentine Clatteaux was a simple country girl from Lorraine who married Paul Delait, baker at Thaon-les-Vosges, at twenty. The town was growing and the Delaits opened a café, which Clémentine ran.

One historic Whitsun, the young couple went to a fair at Nancy, where a sparsely bearded lady was in the sideshow. Later, when café patrons praised this spurious star, Clémentine was evidently seized by feminine jealousy, and she bet five hundred francs that she could raise a better beard.

Clémentine stopped shaving. "I saw it," she recalled, "growing slowly and filling out, and I felt proud and happy. The hairs, of an impeccable chestnut, matched my hair and became soft and lightly waved. Paul, my husband, was visibly moved, and caressed it." The bet was won (though never paid) and Mme Delait became famous.

Fame did not give her a swelled head. She remained a companionable, simple woman, jolly and mysteriously attractive (a local gendarme fell in love with her and another man had her portrait tattooed on his chest), though frightening to some. In 1903 she entered a lions' cage at Epinal. The lions were terrified.

Success made Clémentine, always a nice woman, even nicer. Instead of making a fortune through selling her photograph, she stayed at the café (and found her beard useful for scaring drunks). Her adopted daughter, who adored Mme Delait, describes her mother's dainty feet and well-turned ankle. An eminent professor, Dr. Edgar Bérillon, gave a more detailed description.

"She likes sewing, but prefers delicate needlework, such as embroidery and crochet, in which she displays exquisite taste and remarkable skill. She dresses elegantly. . . . The beard, which is full and heavy, envelops completely the lower part of her face. It divides itself naturally in two, and spreads across her bosom.

"As she herself says, there is probably no bearded lady in the world as strong, as well built and as well proportioned as she is. Her health is always good. . . . Our colleague informs us that her sexual organs are normal. She is naturally cheerful, like all people of excellent health. Mme Delait is the perfect example of a bearded lady."

In 1928, Paul Delait died and Mme Delait and her daughter took up traveling. (Her passport laconically states—under "special markings"—"wears a beard.") She became an attraction in London and Paris, still unmoved by fame.

"Why are people turning around?" she once asked her daughter.

"It's your beard, Mama."

"Well, haven't they ever seen a beard before?"

The years passed. The daughter married a charming man in Epinal and Mme Delait, by now a graybeard, lived happily with them. On April 19, 1939, her exemplary life came to an end, an event recorded on page one of *Paris-Soir*.

On her deathbed, Clémentine showed one last little touch of vanity. "In paradise, I'll wager there's not a beard as fine as mine," she sighed, and she expressed a wish that her tomb be marked, "Here lies Mme Delait, the Bearded Lady of Thaon."

Thirty years later, this wish has finally been realized, and Thaon has also opened a museum in honor of its beloved Clémentine Delait.

April 3, 1969

THE 2 CV: THEY LAUGHED,
THEN LOVED IT

PARIS—They all laughed when Citroën brought out its 2 CV, or two-horsepower, car at the Paris automobile show of 1948: the president of the republic, Vincent Auriol, looks stupefied in a photograph standing by the contraption that was to be described as an umbrella on four wheels, and apparently he uttered only one word, or sound, "Hmm."

In 1995, five years after the last 2 CV had rolled off the assembly line, the newly elected president, Jacques Chirac, who had previously been described as a bulldozer, was asked which car resembled him the most and astutely replied, "A 2 CV."

By then the 2 CV had entered French mythology, lovable, reliable, singular, "a phenomenon where the heart is as strong as reason," a French journalist wrote. "No point in talking of its ugliness," he added. "One doesn't ask Madame Curie or La Pasio-naria to do a striptease." The 2 CV had all the qualities the French admire in themselves including seductiveness if not beauty. "One reason people love it is because it never tried to se-duce and that is the height of coquetry—to seduce without try-ing," says Jacques Wolgensinger, the author of a new book on the 2 CV published by Gallimard, *La 2 CV: Nous nous sommes tant aimés* (The 2 CV: We Loved Each Other So Much).

If the 2 CV was not the first people's car, still it was like no other popular vehicle, says Wolgensinger, who became Citroën's first press attaché in 1957. "The big difference is that the others wanted to be real cars, with solid bodies and a range of colors. They were less spacious inside than the 2 CV and you couldn't take out their back seats and put in a piano."

The father of the 2 CV was Pierre Boulanger who, irritated by horse-drawn wagons that slowed him down while driving along country roads in search of walnut oil, imagined an easily main-tained car for farmers, less road-hogging than a wagon if just as slow. "No faster than a horse," he instructed his engineers.

He also instructed them to be "sordidly economical" and, it is said, demanded a car that could transport eggs over a plowed field without breaking them and accommodate a driver wearing a top hat. (The top hat part sounds apocryphal and was, according to Wolgensinger: A fedora would do.)

Early designs included a motor that would start with a pulled string, like a lawn mower (the final version had a crank instead), a body made from tar paper and, for the 2 CV's single headlight, illumination by fireflies rather than a lightbulb.

The enduring aim of the 2 CV was to be so simple that anyone could repair it with a piece of wire or even string. "Many cars had problems with head gaskets," Wolgensinger says. "The solution was simply not to have any." Likewise with the distributor. For many years the 2 CV had no gas gauge (owners were provided with a dipstick) but it had a roll-back cloth top, making it the world's cheapest convertible.

After forty-nine prototypes, the 2 CV won government approval in August 1939, but production was halted for fear of the car falling into startled enemy hands. So it was not until 1948 that the 2 CV was unveiled. *"Merde alors,* it's ugly," was one recorded comment.

Rather than tar paper, the body was made of metal at least as strong as tin foil. The only available color was gray (blue was soon added, as well as a second headlight); the suspension was as supple as a trampoline. The first ad for the car, overseen by Boulanger, emphasized that it was for farmers, not for the young or for those who wished to climb hills. By the 1960s, the advertising emphasis, Wolgensinger says, was that this minimal car was more than a car: It was a servant, a family friend, a way of life, an enhancer of the soul.

To show its robustness, the 2 CV went on immense transcontinental journeys, three of them (to Afghanistan, Persepolis and from Abidjan to Tunis) organized by Wolgensinger. It also participated in the Monte Carlo rally and the Mille Miglia, and it was converted into a motorboat on pontoons, a sailboat and even an aircraft. By 1958 it had acquired directional signals and from 1976 it appeared in various customized models.

Brigitte Bardot had one, a dance teacher in Toulon covered hers in plush so that passersby could caress it. The farmers for whom it had been designed were outnumbered by those for whom a 2 CV spelled anticonformism. "It wasn't for those who wanted speed, chrome and standing but it gave a sense of friendship to its user," Wolgensinger says.

Unfortunately, speed and chrome and standing, rather than friendship, became what people wanted and also there were new safety and pollution laws. Sales declined from 1977 and the last 2 CV was produced in a plant in Portugal in 1990. The world

grieved along with the French and the 2 CV remains a symbol of France. Last August, in protest against French nuclear tests, Norwegians blew one up in front of the French Embassy in Oslo.

To Wolgensinger, the 2 CV is much more than an automobile. "It is," he says, "the spiritual daughter of Mother Courage and Tom Thumb."

February 3, 1996

AGE-RATED FRENCH ENCYCLOPEDIA
ON SEX

PARIS—The French do it, Lord knows, but hard as this may be for foreigners to believe, they apparently don't know much about it. The laws on contraception are unclear, there are only five family planning centers in all France, French regulations on abortion are on the level with those of Italy, Portugal and Spain, and the Ministry of Education has given no sign that sex education will be added to the school curriculum.

But French children need no longer believe they were born in cabbages: for the first time, a five-volume *Encyclopédie de la Vie Sexuelle* has just come out, written by four physicians and a sociologist and divided by volume according to age group: Vol. I for 7–9 years olds, Vol. II for 10–13 years olds, Vol. III for 14–16 years olds, Vol. IV for 17–18 year olds. The last volume is for adults and was described straight-facedly by one of its authors as an attempt at *recyclage* (job retraining).

The books range in price from fifteen francs for Vol. I to thirty-five francs for the Vol. V refresher course, and are heavily illustrated not only by the usual fateful meetings between sperm and egg, but also by kinky Asiatic artworks and by an inspirational photograph of Sarah Bernhardt in the section on the menopause ("Menopause should no longer be considered as the threshold of old age and the beginning of resignation. . . . Sarah Bernhardt, admirably courageous, still performed on the stage after the amputation of a leg. Is she not an example to us all?").

Understandably moved by the appearance of the encyclopedia, the soundly commercial and not greatly venturesome publishing house of Hachette has ordered two printings of 25,000 and a third is planned. They also invited the books' authors and a large group of journalists and educators to a press conference spread over the Topaz, Agate and Onyx rooms of the glassy new PLM St. Jacques Hotel.

The impeccable arrangements included name tags for everyone, press kits, a rostrum for the authors with a drawing board no one used and a pitcher of iced water (ditto), cries of *plus fort* (louder) and, on the whole, a sympathetic reception for books that are evidently so sorely needed.

Even criticism was sometimes merely disguised praise: "These books are so well done that our children will know everything about sex and nothing about anything else," one lady observed. Another disagreed slightly:

"Fourteen-year-olds can't even remember the names of the rivers of France. How are they going to remember some of the words you use?"

Someone spoke of harmony and of sex being part of the total educational experience. Applause.

One burly man of philosophical bent had a serious criticism to make: so much straight-talking took the romance out of sex.

"The books don't mention pleasure," he pointed out. "They are truly prophylactic in their discussions of frigidity and venereal disease." Perhaps the encyclopedia was too explicit? There was a thoughtful silence until one of the encyclopedia's illustrators leapt to his feet with an argument any Frenchman would understand:

"Just because I know how a Poulet Marengo is made," he said, "does not prevent me from enjoying it." Much applause.

A lady with a ponytail, leaning earnestly forward in her seat, explained that she had driven over hundred kilometers to voice her objection: the books speak of leaving the joyous world of childhood and entering the *triste* adult world. This, the lady stated, was a sign of corrosive pessimism and she for one didn't find the adult world *triste*. Perhaps, she added, she felt this way because she lived in the provinces. The Parisians in the audiences nodded smugly: all Parisians know, and take great joy in the fact, that *la vie* is very *triste*.

The weakest sections of the encyclopedia are on psychology, and the books' specialist in psychology was least able to explain himself.

"How can your book state that stealing a car is a mere peccadillo, that the person who does so is not a thief?" inquired one indignant lady.

"The adolescent has no sense of property," answered the expert. "In stealing a car he is trying to get the phallus he has not yet acquired." The expert did not add, as he did in the book, that in addition to symbolizing the paternal penis, the automobile represents the nestlike comfort of the maternal womb, but he may as well have.

"A *histoire* of a phallus because someone steals a car," muttered an indignant voice. The audience rumbled in agreement.

"Why in your book is homosexuality listed as a perversion?" a voice asked. "Perversion is not a pejorative word to us," the expert answered finely. "Homosexuals are just narcissists trying to find the exact reflections of themselves in their partners."

"So are many heterosexuals," a voice shot back. Slight rumble.

There was discussion on whether the coupling models in the

illustrations should have been wearing wedding rings or not and the inevitable question, will the working class read these books, seconded and brought more up to date by another voice asking, will immigrants read these books.

"It is," proclaimed a well-known woman journalist, "reactionary to think that only the rich are interested in intelligent things." Applause, and smiles from the man from Hachette.

Conversation was still going strong when it was announced that luncheon would now be served. Regrettably, this columnist did not stick around to see if the menu included Poulet Marengo.

May 5, 1973

LUMINOUS IDEAS
OF THE CONCOURS LÉPINE

PARIS—One of the rites of spring here is the small corner at the huge Foire de Paris where inventors display their brainchildren at the Concours Lépine in the hope of finding buyers, backers or just someone to talk to.

Each year, under the aegis of the Association des Inventeurs et Fabricants Français, there are new and better coat hangers, burglar alarms, vegetable choppers and mashers, stain removers (although, alas, no longer the reversible necktie in case the remover doesn't work). There is always an improved oyster opener and, this year, a tented bed whose draperies cunningly conceal a 750-kilogram (1,650-pound) metal armature, available in twin, queen and king sizes, to protect the sleeper during an earthquake.

This year's competition, just over, attracted 160 inventors, including a contingent from China that showed not only a traditional Concours Lépine entry, magnetic socks to combat foot odor, but a device to protect against mobile telephone fraud, flameproof cables, electronic window cleaners, denim sneakers, a fake coin detector and Madame Wang Tong's dermatological application of acupuncture, which has cured more than thirty thousand acne sufferers (names of satisfied customers available if you want to telephone China).

Named after Louis Lépine, the Paris police prefect who founded it in 1902, the concours attracts eccentrics, hustlers and dreamers to whom invention is the mother of necessity.

Wishing to emphasize the positive, the organizers annually point out that it was at the Concours Lépine that the world first saw the ballpoint pen (1919), the pressure cooker (1926), the dirigible (1908), the steam iron (1921), the creped-sole shoe (1927) and contact lenses (1948). The list notes that in not all cases did the inventor gain the fortune and fame that was his due.

One who did was the late Jean Mantelet who in 1932 won a prize for the vegetable masher that he commercialized under the soon-to-be world famous name of Moulinex. "There are always people with luminous ideas. They are not in the majority," Mantelet told *Inventions* magazine in 1967.

This year's exhibitors were perhaps less illuminated than the inventors of a substance to replace rain, the method of playing Ping-Pong by oneself, or the benefactor of humanity who gave his secret for preventing car thefts to anyone who would stop to listen: Just take the accelerator with you when you leave your car.

Practical devices this year included tires easily fitted on wheelchairs so they can be used on the beach and a way of converting motorbikes into mobile first-aid units. But there were still a few exhibitors combining the White Knight's practicality with the persistence of the Ancient Mariner. There was the lady hawking water-filled inner soles whose sales spiel—"hammer toes . . . varicose veins . . . back pain but not slipped disks"—continued long

after the listener had disappeared into the crowd, and then there was the burly figure of Charles Anastassiades, a Greek-born tailor.

Anastassiades has invented a way of attaching buttons to shirts without sewing them on. He has already won a prize for this, so why did he come back this year?

"Because I have improved it." Anastassiades went on to explain his philosophy of life, which happens often enough at the Concours Lépine, and then demanded, "Madame, you who are a journalist, perhaps you can tell me this: Why do people claim that Macedonia is not Greek?" In a quieter corner was the young inventor of a large black-and-white beach ball that splits to reveal a spill-proof bar complete with bottles and glasses. Perfected in 1990, it has, sadly, yet to attract a backer. In another booth Michel Perucca and Rafi Abrilian were showing their first inventions, a heel protector for automobilists' shoes and a cane equipped with a tripod in which it can rest when not needed.

Gaetan Guibert, who has a neatly parted beard and a sweet smile, won a medal at the Concours Lépine in 1979 and has shown at other fairs. "The ideas just come," he says. A former stonecutter and beach photographer, he invented a device to glue wallpaper to the ceiling and this year is showing a sort of motorized brush-equipped pole to remove asbestos from buildings.

With asbestos detection and removal now mandatory in France, Guibert thinks he is on the cusp of success even if he hasn't had a chance to try out his prototype on an asbestos-laced site. "I know it will work," he says. He has made contacts but found no buyers.

This year, the Association des Inventeurs put the Concours Lépine on the Internet and gave it an e-mail address, which should encourage a lot of the participants, although not Gaetan Guibert. He doesn't have a computer.

"Oh no," he said. "I don't understand such things at all."

May 10, 1997

ASSEMBLY LINE VACATIONS

PARIS—Just because the major portion of the French population is about to hit the road for the long summer vacation that became law in 1936, there is no reason to expect a carefree or joyful mood. Indeed, there is always a perhaps pleasurable frisson of anxiety about *les grandes vacances*.

"Vacations more expensive than ever this year," says a wet-blanket headline in *Le Matin,* while another paper warns "Beware of the open air" and *Paris-Match* suggests that local water be analyzed before vacationers drink it or bathe in it. *Le Nouvel Observateur* recounts a reporter's futile quest for a free beach along the Côte d'Azur, while the Ministry of Health has rushed out a pamphlet on what to do if you find a place to stretch out in the sun: spend as little time in it as possible.

To suit the mood, a French bank has brought out a 323-page

guidebook of consummate weirdness. It is called the *Guide Société Générale du Tourisme Technique* and it recommends that vacationers spend their time off visiting factories.

Tourists may visit the biggest sawmill in the east of France and even a factory where, it is promised, "all the secrets of galvanization will be revealed." Vacationing housewives can relax at factories that produce kitchen stoves, aprons and vegetable peelers and can even watch household garbage being processed quite near Paris, at Nanterre.

A busman might wish to take a busman's holiday at the Etablissements Compin in Normandy, which makes seats not only for buses but for trains as well. A post office employee would surely find it worth the detour to Bourganeuf in the Creuse where, since 1960, forty-five people have been employed in the manufacture of mailmen's uniforms.

The guidebook is not to be taken lightly. It is an effort to "promote the new face of modern France," according to Jean-Pierre Soisson, the French minister of sports and leisure, who wrote its preface.

"Here at the end of the twentieth century," Soisson says, "it is evident that one can love Romanesque churches and at the same time wish to visit a factory using the most advanced techniques. . . . It is normal that one should stop in a region rich in museums, chateaux or historical monuments, but also that one should wish to discover an ultramodern nuclear energy plant or a tidal power station unique in France."

Sure. And one can also visit factories that make: razor blades, suitcases, Louis XV furniture, ladies' undergarments, hair dyes, nightshirts, tractors, bugles, stencils, shawls, cheese, noodles, skis, fire extinguishers, foam rubber and animal feed.

For those who are sick of cathedral spires, there is a factory that makes sugar from beets and boasts an inspiring sugar tower twenty-one meters high. (At another sugar factory all the offices are circular, or beet-shaped.) Why waste money taking holiday pictures when you can visit a photo-processing lab instead? Instead of playing cards on the beach, why not spend an edifying afternoon watching playing cards being made (thirty thousand decks a day!) in the Gironde? Is there a lazier occupation than watching the grass grow? Yes: watching the wines age (it takes three years) in a warehouse in the Pyrenées.

Those with a sense of tradition would probably want to watch the making of such Old World products as Sèvres porcelain, Roquefort cheese, cider, cough drops, Cointreau, Champagne or calvados. Modern minds will enjoy watching plastic film being extruded in the Pas-de-Calais, while those with a taste for puns will be irresistibly drawn to a truck builder in the Loiret called Toutenkamion.

While Montélimar seems to concentrate solely on its famous nougats, the town of Aubusson is interesting not only for its tapestry manufactures but for its lightbulb factories. The guidebook is also good at offering itineraries. After visiting the Montbazillac distillery in the Dordogne, why not go on to Mouleydier, a village brutally martyred in World War II, and then see the hydroelectric dam at Tuileries?

For vacationers who head for popular resorts willy-nilly, a word of advice. Don't just sit at the racetrack at Deauville, inspect the iron mines at nearby Caen as well. While on the Côte d'Azur do not neglect the noisome industrial complex of Fos, much as you would like to. Try to specialize, say, in mines (potassium, talc) or in paper (carbon, corrugated or waxed, which is made from a pulp oddly called *pâte de charme*).

For a really different holiday, watch simulated road accidents at the Peugeot factory instead of real ones on the *autoroute*. According to the guidebook, at least two slaughterhouses are open to the curious, and it also lists, and recommends for schoolchildren, an assembly line on which chickens are killed according to the most modern methods.

It is, as Soisson says in his preface, a way to understand our times, though that would seem to be the last thing anyone would want to do while on holiday. There seems, however, to be one flaw in this earnest book and that is that it neglects the frivolous fact of the *fermeture annuelle*. So, while anxious tourists are lining up to see rubber vulcanized, dies cut or chickens eviscerated, the workers who perform these tasks the year long may well have locked up shop, piled into their cars and headed for the sea, sun, siestas and the other inconsequential pleasures of *les vacances*.

July 28, 1979

FRENCH PURSUING
THE RIGHT NUMBER

PARIS—There is always a terrific amount of art news in Paris in the autumn, and this year offers the bonus of the big Impressionist show. So heated is the pace, in fact, that the National Archives have thoughtfully prepared an exhibit on Louis-Philippe—a French king noted for his pear shape, general dreariness and habit of carrying an umbrella—that should be as soothing as six Valiums to the fevered art lover.

This preface is really by way of an excuse for not writing earlier about a show that has just closed but drew such crowds that it seems worth mentioning even after the fact. It was an outdoor show on the Left Bank, held in an area roughly situated between the Rodin Museum and Calder's UNESCO stabile, and it was devoted to telephone booths. Telephone booths, seventeen of them, from eight countries! And, despite the icy cold and rain, the crowds were dense.

There were people opening booth doors, testing dialing mechanisms, discussing form and color and carefully noting their opinions on ballots provided by the Ministry of Posts and Telecommunications, which sponsored the show.

"The prime quality sought for a telephone booth is aesthetic," a ministry bulletin explains. "It must suit the environment, its transparence must give a sense of lightness, its windows must be easy to clean and offer visibility to discourage malefactors."

"What I seek in a telephone booth," said a man in a porkpie hat who was making very careful notes, "is spaciousness and rationality and a sense of isolation." His favorite was No. 10, a French model 2.19 meters tall with the stark word TELEPHONE written across its top and a price tag of 1,350 francs plus tax. The man in the porkpie hat went into the booth and pretended to dial. It looked like a swell booth, all right.

Tastes differ. A lot of art lovers liked a yellow German booth that had an ashtray, but one woman noted you could get squeezed in the door. A capacious Swiss model that could easily have held a cow, milkmaid and milking stool was judged spartan because it had no shelf for packages. There were many arguments over whether Sweden's or Britain's doors worked the best, and no one much liked the models that exposed the user's ankles to the winds.

Visitors' ballots were secret, but some urgent investigative reporting in the ministry's office on the exhibition site revealed that Belgium, Germany and France were ahead.

The ministry's office also had some fine artwork on its wall—things that light up when pressed, and graphs about telephones, tastefully mounted against a picture of the Eiffel Tower. There were also many brochures, including one that showed a man in silhouette gesticulating furiously toward the mouthpiece of a public telephone. Perhaps that wasn't the artist's intention, but that's what one most often sees French telephone users doing.

The reason for an exhibition of public telephone booths is of course quite simple: It's so wretchedly hard in France to get a phone of one's own. Only 22 percent of French homes have telephones and the average waiting time, once one has applied for one, is over a year.

Real estate agents have been known to gull prospective tenants by putting dummy phones in flats, and an employee of this paper had her telephone snatched away to be put, she is sure, in the new Maine Montparnasse office complex. According to an angry consumer group, the Association Française des Utilisateurs du Téléphone et des Télécommunications (AFUTT), some two million French people were waiting for telephones last year.

Further, it costs almost four times as much to make a local telephone call in Paris as Madrid. The monthly rental fee in Paris is about $6 as against $3 in New York and the installation fee is less than $15 in New York and over $100 in Paris. Worst, the French government often asks an advance payment of $500 before it will consider installing a telephone.

Clearly incapable of meeting private needs, the government plans to start putting public booths on Paris streets at a rhythm of about hundred a month starting in January. Pleasing and lovely as the chosen booths will undoubtedly be, will they be attractive on Paris streets? The enthusiastic man in the porkpie hat, for example, hadn't exactly envisaged a telephone booth on *his* street.

"No, no, no," he said, "not my street. Where I think they should be is in public squares so if a child gets sick a mother can call the doctor. Public squares, that's the place for them."

The Ministry of Posts and Telecommunications offers, in addition to its stunning display of prospective telephone booths, lots of statistics about cables being laid and the chances, vastly improved it appears, that one now has of actually getting one's call through. There are great plans for automation, none too soon for, according to AFUTT, France in this point ranks ninety-eighth in the world, tied with Nigeria but well behind Zambia, Portugal and Mongolia.

So, France may be lacking in telephones (one desperate Parisian even thought of buying a small car and putting it in his apartment, as car telephones are comparatively easy to get, but reason prevailed and, after two and a half years of waiting, he got an ordinary phone), but thanks to this recent show Paris may soon have the best-looking public telephone booths in Europe, and that's something. Isn't it?

October 19, 1974

Twenty-five years after this piece appeared, there were so many private telephones in France, including 20 million cellular telephones, that public cabins were being removed throughout the country on the grounds that they were no longer needed.

HOW LONG IS LONG?
THE METER TURNS 200

PARIS—To each its own measure, said the classical precept, sententious as such precepts often are. What does measure mean? How long is long, how full is a cup? It is a question the French brooded on even before they declared themselves Cartesian and therefore capable of solving life's mysteries through logic: Charlemagne, Charles the Bald, François I and Henri II all tried to find a universal system of measurement and failed.

Then, in 1795, the metric system was adopted, "well-suited to the dignity of the French people," though apparently not to the British, who had been invited to share in the great discovery but refused to benefit from this landmark of revolutionary rationality. "France has been called upon to conquer the universal measure," an engineer informed the Convention in 1793. An earlier attempt to decimalize the day by dividing it into 10 hours of 100 minutes composed of 100 seconds had proved too logical to work.

The bicentenary of the metric system, allowing weights and measures to be meted out on a simple decimal system, is being celebrated by a rather mingy exhibition at the noble Archives de France, on whose terrace some of the triangulations leading to the new system were noted. The center of the show is the standard meter, a slim bar in platinum, the metal least subject to alteration by heat or cold. It was the standard from which copies were made, and the fact that it is 0.2 millimeters shorter than it should be (and the standard kilo was later proved to be 27 milligrams too heavy) does not diminish its value.

Other standard meters were engraved on public buildings including one that can still be seen at the entrance to the Ministry of Justice on the Place Vendôme.

Until the meter came along there were hundreds of systems of measurement in use in France, some based on the human body, like the *pied* (foot), some on units of time (a day's work), some on means of transport (a barrel, a sack). The foot came in 20 varieties depending on the region, a day's work had 40 different meanings simply in the Moselle area, the land measure known as an *arpent* was different for royal forests and of course favorable to the king. Fabrics followed different measures according to whether they were wool or silk, a parquet floor was measured in *toises* while the carpet that covered it was measured in *aunes*.

How to make sense of all this? Perhaps to find a measure based on the swinging of a pendulum, people thought in 1670, but this turned out to be easier on paper than in reality. The solution was to measure the arc of the meridian from Dunkerque to Barcelona, deduce from this the length of the entire meridian from the North Pole to the Equator and declare the meter to be equal to one ten-millionth of a quarter of that distance.

Somehow this was found both comprehensible and acceptable and France had a whole new system of measurement giving a

fixed relation between the unit of length, the meter, and units of capacity and weight, the liter and the kilogram.

The people hated it.

If, according to Condorcet, the new system assured the Rights of Man by uniform and equitable measurements, citizens preferred the system they were used to, even if people who understood about meridians said the old ways were "gothic and barbaric." The new system offered new ways of cheating the unwary, eased by the fact that the official standards of meters, kilos and liters were often delivered to the provinces years after they became law.

Later, inspectors were sent to the provinces to ensure that the new system was being followed. They were weighed down by 30 kilos of measuring material but had neither official uniforms nor the authority to fine wrongdoers.

Charts of the new measurements were distributed and mnemonics suggested for new words. By 1832, when people were still having trouble, a new rational five-franc coin appeared: It weighed 25 grams and its diameter was 37 millimeters. Forty of the pieces would equal 1 kilo, and 27 pieces laid side by side would be a meter, or almost. Very logical but not that many people had 27 or 40 five-franc pieces to pile up or lay out side by side.

Before that, Napoléon, cottoning on to the public's confusion because he shared it, allowed some of the old words for weights and measures to be revived and during the Restoration the metric system was abolished in retail trade.

It was reinstated from 1840 and this time the inspectors were given fine uniforms and the right to charge offenders.

From an interesting philosophical problem, the metric system had become a political football, an economic tool and a vehicle of national pride: "All the people of Europe admire and envy the French system of weights and measures," it was proclaimed and in time about 180 countries adopted it.

But not all of the French. The exhibition includes displays of daily goods that contravene the 1795 law which stated that double and half-kilos and liters are acceptable, but not quarters and eighths. Yet butter is commonly sold today in 125- or 250-gram packets and beer by *"demis"* of 33 centiliters. French-made gloves follow inch-sizes as do faucets, while sailors use nautical miles and knots.

The exhibition at the Archives Nationales is called Le Mal de Changer and change does not come lightly here. The "new" franc, for example, came into existence in 1960 but many French men and women still count in old francs, including those not even born thirty-five years ago.

June 24, 1995

THE "RUSTPROOF" CANDIDATE
FOR THE FRENCH PRESIDENCY

PARIS—While the putative major runners in this spring's French presidential elections executed a pussyfooting pavane, one candidate stepped forward early. Asked during a radio interview last month whether she would be a candidate, Arlette Laguiller replied, "*évidemment*" (obviously). It is her fourth try.

Arlette Laguiller, the rustproof, as *Le Monde* calls her, candidate of Lutte Ouvrière, will have a score of 3 percent in the first round of the election, according to a poll in the conservative magazine *Le Point*. This is only about one-tenth of the major, if undeclared, contestants, but it is still an estimated one million votes. Not bad for a Trotskyite office worker who preaches revolution, believes the profit motive to be inherently evil and considers elections more an opiate than an instrument of change.

A dangerous woman? Apparently not at all. At her best, with

her simplicity and concern about social issues ("the other candidates talk about them every seven years when the elections come up. I talk about them all the time"), she can come across as a breath of fresh air amid the windy discourse of politicians in gray suits.

The French do not love their policitians, clever though they are, but they are clearly—though maybe patronizingly—affectionate toward Arlette as she is always called. It is impossible to imagine people speaking of François or Jacques or Lionel. "I think it is affection or the fact that people think me accessible," she says. "People who don't like me don't call me Arlette."

Arlette, fifty-four, has only about two thousand members in Lutte Ouvrière, or Workers' Struggle, and generally resurfaces to the public's fleeting attention only during presidential campaigns. The rest of the time she works for the party, writes a weekly editorial in its newspaper and is an employee at the Crédit Lyonnais bank, where she began as a typist at the age of sixteen earning 230 francs a month.

"I am not a worker, I have never dirtied my hands except to change a typewriter ribbon," she says. "But I am a member of the working class." She sees no contradiction in a Trotskyite working in a bank.

"It is better to understand and denounce capitalism from its center," she said over a Perrier in a café across the street from the bank's monumental nineteenth-century headquarters with its architectural references to the Parthenon, Gothic cathedrals, Karnak and the Château of Chambord.

She is a small, doughty and extremely—almost professionally—pleasant woman. She is accorded the sometimes dismissive sympathy the French reserve for those they consider naive. "So picturesque, *la petite femme populo*," says a resident of the aristocratic seventh arrondissement.

The French electoral system is based on two rounds: In the first people traditionally vote on the basis of mischief or ideals, in the second they get real. Arlette has never reached the second round, but for the first round she can be a comfortable choice. Ecologists cause qualms, Communists bore, cranks do not amuse a Cartesian mind. Arlette reminds the French of how tolerant they are. Her political program may be about as realistic as John Lennon's "Imagine," but she is decent, homespun and, above all, harmless.

"Arlette is part of our national heritage," a banker proclaims. "She is like cassoulet."

She is in her way comforting: reliable in her candidacies and a reminder of the hope-filled nineteenth-century radical past (there is hardly a French city that does not have a street named after the slain socialist leader Jean Jaurès, and it was, after all, a Frenchman who composed the Internationale). That she is committed to the principle of permanent revolution seems not to trouble anyone, and even Arlette does not believe the revolution will occur just now.

"I wouldn't say we are on the eve of the revolution," she says, but this does not mean she considers the struggle vain. "Voltaire's ideas influenced the French Revolution although he didn't live to see it."

In the present state of unease about unemployment and corruption in French business and politics, Arlette has chosen as a central issue to argue that corporations should be obliged to open their books to the public so that claims that firings are economically necessary can be investigated: "They can fork out for bribes, why not for salaries?" the party newspaper asks.

Arlette's first candidacy, in 1974, followed her successful involvement in a bank employees' strike that year, which in turn followed the fugitive joys of the mini-uprising of 1968. She began militating in 1960, for Algerian independence, and when she ran for president in 1974 *Le Figaro* insultingly advised her to stick to her typewriter and remember her place.

Lutte Ouvrière is one of three French Trotskyite parties. This may be Arlette Laguiller's fourth election but she seems startled when asked if she actually wants to be president.

"Do you mean would I accept if there was a revolution? Of course, but I don't think I'll be chosen unless the masses express their will other than in the voting booth. I can't see Lutte Ouvrière being at the head of the country and the bourgeoisie allowing it to happen. I may be a candidate but I know perfectly well that it's not the elections that will change the country."

Then why bother running? "To address a wider public—elections have a different resonance than the militants' daily grind—and to show that there are people who want change even if they know an election won't bring it. I am not afraid our party will fade away but I do think we should have a word in the debate in order to show resistance, small perhaps but big rivers come from small streams. Everyone knows that."

Come the revolution and the dictatorship of the proletariat, the workers of the world will unite and the former members of the ruling classes will, it is a consoling thought, not necessarily lose their political rights. But right now the river isn't a stream and certainly not a freshet. Does Arlette have a personal motto? Yes, she does: *"Tenez bon,"* she says, hang on.

November 26, 1994

In the presidential election, won by Jacques Chirac, Arlette scored a record 1.6 million voters, or about 5 percent of the total. By 1998, her party had for the first time won seats in the regional elections, twenty of them including one for Arlette, who soon after posed in her living room for a celebrity magazine. In 1999 the party won five seats in the European parliament. "Arlette has become chic," the daily newspaper *Libération* noted.

VIRTUOSI OF THE PEOPLE'S PIANO

PARIS—The really big recording artists of France are not the really big international names. Instead, they are people hardly known outside France: Yvette Horner, André Verchuren, Jo Privat and the man known sweetly only by his surname, Aimable. They play the accordion.

Yvette Horner is the only woman, the biggest seller of all (*Multimillionaire du Disque,* her albums boast), a tiny brunette with a gummy smile and a tall pompadour who lives in a mansion where as many furnishings as possible (including the fireplace) are accordion-shaped. Like the other accordionists she is almost always on the road. In Alsace she was Queen of Sauerkraut. She has also been declared Queen of Spain, a title sadly diminished by its affix, ". . . of the Six-Day Bicycle Races." Although Aimable is considered the most popular accordionist in the north of France, Yvette's

"Song of the Miners" is so loved there that a bunch of miners, it is said, once lay in the road in front of her car and she was unable to proceed without favoring them with a chorus or two. "The accordion is life, the accordion is glory," Yvette has remarked.

In France the accordion is known as the piano of the poor, or the *piano à bretelles* (piano with suspenders). It is the instrument of that near-mythical entity called *le peuple*, which usually means someone else except for moments when it is prudent to show one's own earthy roots. Former President Valéry Giscard d'Estaing, who was not famous for being one of the people, once sought to court popularity by playing the old squeeze box. "He played '*Je Cherche la Fortune*,' an old Aristide Bruant song, and not at all badly," Jo Privat says.

Privat is one of the grand old names of the accordion, one of the three Jos who gave his name to the Balajo on the rue de Lappe near the Bastille—once a center for *apaches* and *bal-musette* and now, Privat says sadly, largely given over to disco music. Privat has very black hair and the build of a furniture mover slightly stooped from decades of wearing *le piano à bretelles*.

He is one of the stars of the international accordion festival, an annual rite of spring that is being held this year in several working-class suburbs of Paris. Participants include tango accordionists, the American jazz accordionist Art Van Damme and a classical accordionist from Russia, Viatcheslav Semionov. Privat and his orchestra and vocalist Muriel—*la Môme du Balajo* (the Balajo Kid)—will play on May 20 at Bobigny and on May 26 at the Parc Départemental of Bagnolet.

According to the accordion expert Clément Lepidis, Privat is more authentic than such celebrated rivals as Horner and Aimable (who are not appearing in the festival) because they play anything, while he is the last remaining specialist of *bal-musette*. The word *musette*, according to Lepidis, came about because around 1900 some Auvergnats appeared on the rue de Lappe playing a bagpipelike instrument called the *musette*.

The music of the *bal-musette,* Lepidis says, is better heard than described. You dance the *java* and slow waltz to it although, Privat adds sadly, "Sometimes we play rock now. One must keep up with the times."

There used to be 350 *bals-musettes* in France, says Lepidis, thirty or forty of them in Paris. Now there are four or five. The accordion, he says, was invented in 1829 by a German of Armenian origin and many of the greatest accordionists are Italian. Privat's family was Italian although he was raised in the tough Ménilmontant area of Paris, where Maurice Chevalier was born.

No instrument is more French, more nostalgic for old days when there were *apaches* and *mauvais garçons* and their *gonzesses* (molls) and everyone was tough and loving. One of Privat's big hits is a 1925 song called *"Les Bouges,"* argot for ill-frequented places, as his eighteen-year-old vocalist, Muriel, genteelly explains. She sings in straightforward style, sometimes with her hand in her pockets. "You must be simple, you have to have the soul of the people to sing these songs," she says.

Berg, Hindemith and Schoenberg have used the accordion but it remains an instrument that is, in the word's widest meaning, popular. Objectively, the music it makes is quite awful (a dog expert says never to leave the radio on when you go out: If an accordion comes on, the dog will yowl forever), and yet the echo of an accordion in a Métro corridor makes going to work mornings bearable.

The accordion is easy to dislike and hard to resist. At the press conference for the accordion festival, a handful of journalists in an ugly room listened to someone read aloud the schedule they already held in their hands. The torpor could have been cut with a knife. Then someone struck up an air on the accordion and suddenly, and very briefly, people danced a slow waltz.

May 18, 1984

FRENCH HISTORY:
PAST AND PRESENT CLASH

PARIS—France is a religion, the historian Michelet famously said. And so like every faith it must have its feasts, schisms and commemorations, especially its schisms and commemorations. Each year, the National Archive publishes a booklet of people and events to be feted, the criterion, according to its editor, Elisabeth Pauly, being their importance in the history of France.

This year's list is the usual mixed bag—the four hundredth birthday of Descartes, the centenaries of Artaud, Tzara and André Breton—all savantly chosen to give even the smallest municipality and overseas territory an excuse for a subsidized cultural clambake. Some years there is a ruckus: the bicentenary of the French Revolution, for example, and the tricentenary, in 1985, of the revocation of the Edict of Nantes.

This year the trouble is Clovis (ca. 466–511). And Clovis, to everyone's surprise, has turned out to be very big trouble indeed. What might have been a massive yawn—the event being celebrated is the 1,500th anniversary of his baptism in Reims—has turned into a howl involving the government, the Pope, the media and the unholy National Front leader, Jean-Marie Le Pen who, while everyone else was nattering, co-opted Clovis's anniversary in a torchlight procession to the patch of Latin Quarter asphalt under which the Salian Frankish king is thought to lie.

No one knows much about Clovis, the first account of his life having been written sixty years after his death and with no trace of impartiality by Grégoire de Tours. To most French people he is less real than his fictional though more vivacious predecessor Astérix le Gaulois, but everyone has a schoolbook memory of a fearsome if somehow pious warrior cleaving the head of a soldier who had broken a religious relic, the vase of Soissons (current thinking is that the soldier merely dented it), and opportunely becoming a Catholic.

From Gauls (a word meaning good for nothing, ill educated, sickly), the predominant tribe became Franks, which meant courageous if ill-smelling. A nation, it has been claimed, was born. "Clovis, the Birth of France," is the title of a special issue of a popular history magazine, while the authors of one of the nine books on Clovis published this year say that what is being celebrated is "less the baptism of Clovis than the myth—in the noblest sense of the term—of the baptism of France."

The trouble began early this winter with the announcement of the official commemoration, has risen through the spring and summer (in April, the government named a committee of Clovis overseers) and is expected to reach its height in September when Pope John Paul II goes to Reims to celebrate the baptism.

One of the first criticisms, in *Le Monde*, pointed out the nationalism and anti-multiculturism implicit in the celebration (Clovis has always been considered more "French" than, say, Charlemagne, who was a little too German). But the main argu-

ment has been why is a country in which church and state have been separated since 1905 celebrating a strictly Catholic event on a national scale and spending vast sums to do so.

France, says the historian Pierre Chaunu in *Baptême de Clovis, Baptême de la France,* has passed from a sort of State Catholicism to a sort of State Atheism, in which even the devout Charles de Gaulle never used the word *God* in public, except when abroad. The fact that President Jacques Chirac publicly took communion at the funeral of François Mitterrand and knelt to the pope during a state visit to Rome has riled captious defenders of the secular state. (The Free Masons of France, for example, have announced that they want no part of Clovis year.)

Clovis can never be as ecumenical as Joan of Arc, canonized by the Catholics and respected by Protestants for resisting authority, including that of the bishops who condemned her. Clovis is so much a myth that in a country obsessed with national identity (which often means who can be excluded), the myth is easily appropriated by anyone with an axe to grind.

Literally, an axe: the *francisque,* or axe, with which Clovis struck the soldier who broke the vase of Soissons later became a symbol of Vichy France.

Over the centuries he was seen as the model Christian king (Louis, the most-used Christian name among French kings, comes from Clovis), then as the inventor of a constitutional monarchy, then as an enemy of the revolution (and thus a hero to surviving Royalists), then as a symbol of a Christian, rather than a secular, republic. To some of the most strident opponents of the present celebrations he represents the present government's attempts to win the support of the far right moral majority.

Elisabeth Pauly of the National Archive, who unwittingly started the fuss when in 1991 she thought of making this Clovis's year, defends her choice by saying simply, "The adoption by Clovis of Roman Catholicism was of great consequence to the history of France. That much is beyond dispute." But the dispute is still there. To retaliate against the baptism commemoration, one group is demanding to be de-baptized; others are planning demonstrations during the pope's visit. The umbrella group of protesters is called Clovis Is Not France.

And then there is the question of the date: historians agree that Clovis was baptized on December 25, but the year is another question. Perhaps 498 or 506, but almost certainly not 496.

July 13, 1996

AN ELECTION IN WHICH
THE SCOFFLAW WINS

PARIS—French voters are said to be in a grumpy mood but why is that woman smiling as she steps smartly out of the tiny coupe double-parked in front of the hairdresser's? And that business-man sweeping his Jaguar with a flourish into a bus stop? And that pensioner, so sprightly after saving on four parking tickets at 240 francs (about $50) each?

They do not feel great about the presidential election but they love one of its traditions: an amnesty on parking violations. The last amnesty, after the presidential election of 1988, is said to have cost the state eight billion francs in unpaid fines.

None of the candidates—they do, after all, know which side their ballot is buttered on—came out against the amnesty which also benefits certain misdemeanors and minor offenses and, to ease overcrowded prisons, annuls short-term jail sentences. But in a car-crazy country it is the thought of avoiding a parking fine that seizes the imagination and gives this tightly administered nation an illusion of springtime anarchy.

The amnesty began in 1965, not surprisingly under the illusionless president who knew his fellow citizens better than anyone, Charles de Gaulle. There is no law that says it must be voted into existence after each presidential election, but what president can resist boosting his popularity by giving voters an inauguration gift? People say that the amnesty is *la pommade* (the unguent) to make the new wheels turn.

If no candidate has condemned the amnesty, none has made it part of his or her electoral campaign. So a fictitious but delightfully wicked uncertainty about forgiveness adds spice to a refusal to drop a coin in a parking meter and piques the timidest souls as they edge their wheels into forbidden space. Already, Paris's meter maids, or *pervenches* (periwinkles), as they are called because of their blue uniforms, steel themselves for insults as they reach for their ticket pads.

"You don't even see *pervenches* around these days," claims a jubilant stockbroker. "They've gone into hiding."

Since the amnesty is based more on tradition and executive privilege than on jurisprudence, there is a degree of uncertainty as to how much the automobilist can get away with. Excessive speeds, fatalities and drunken driving are not likely to be forgiven, nor are backlogs of fines to which the country's zealous *huissiers* (bailiffs) have already laid claim. On the other hand, those who have refused to pay parking violations since January—and one-third of the tickets issued have been ignored—are probably perfectly safe.

The amnesty is part of electoral folklore but cheerfully destructive of republican virtues. It annuls decisions made in law courts and demonstrates the monarchic power of the French president who, aided by a compliant Parliament, can erase administrative procedures by simple fiat.

Judges and the police detest the amnesty; the national road safety organization, La Prévention Routière, says that while road accidents are decreasing in France, "the amnesty syndrome" causes an increase in road fatalities before presidential elections.

The French electoral system, with two rounds, operates on the pragmatic view that no candidate is immediately desirable. In the first round, each voter expresses hope or rage; in the second he or she complies with his or her notion of good sense, which rarely includes enthusiasm (the effusions after the 1981 victory of François Mitterand were unique).

It is a system that encourages a strong sense of letdown once the results are in. So for that reason *vive l'amnistie.* In a country where thirty-three million citizens hold driving permits, what it says is that, despite the election results, everyone wins.

April 26, 1995

1944:

THE MANY WHO WERE FORGOTTEN

PARIS—The line between commemoration and celebration and opportunism is easily blurred, as the June 6 anniversary showed (even the French tobacco lobby stepped in with an ad equating the Normandy landings with the freedom to smoke). But this is just a beginning: The coming summer's festivities around the fiftieth anniversary of the liberation of Paris—all by itself, as de Gaulle so flatteringly and inaccurately put it—will undoubtedly further exacerbate France's well-known problems with memory. A good remedy is to read the small memorial notices to resistants and deportees that have been appearing in recent months in *Le Monde*.

In the usual tiny type, flanked by the usual records of deaths and entrances, there have been brief listings of the date and convoy number in which friends and relations were dispatched to death camps fifty years ago. A typical note, in memory of their parents, was signed by Simone Weil, France's minister of health, and her sister.

On the same day, another notice appeared, longer than usual: It was a complicated story told with chilling brevity of the deportation of more than two hundred survivors of the Warsaw ghetto, all of them holding papers that should have guaranteed their freedom had only international charities and foreign governments acted in time. They were shipped from Vittel to the station at Drancy, outside Paris, from which all but seventeen of the seventy-nine trains that carried Jews to their death departed.

In the current officialization of memory, the death of forty-one Jewish children who sought safety in a hostel in Izieu has been declared by President François Mitterrand a symbol of all the Jews exterminated under the Vichy regime. But there were many other now-forgotten children. In Vittel, forty-six were deported, the eldest fourteen years old, the youngest a bare six months.

The memorial notice in *Le Monde* was put there by two former internees in the Vittel camp, Sofka Skipworth, who died before it was printed, and Madeleine White, now the wife of an Auschwitz survivor, the French astronomer Jean-Louis Steinberg.

Madeleine Steinberg, seventy-three, is small and vigorous, passionately precise and perhaps unaware that sometimes as she speaks her eyes fill with tears. Her notice was put in *Le Monde,* like so many others, to remember the unconsidered dead, but this does not make remembering any easier. It took her husband twenty-five years, she says, to be able to talk to her about Auschwitz.

The main internment camp for British women was Vittel, in eastern France. The young Madeleine White and her mother were sent there in May 1941. Although both women considered themselves French, they held British passports because of Mrs. White's romantic and unsuccessful marriage to a World War I veteran.

"At the beginning in Vittel there were only English people, but all sorts," Mrs. Steinberg said. "Women like my mother who had married British soldiers and couldn't face life in England, high-ranking people with British firms, retired nannies, wives of jockeys, lots of dancers, prostitutes who had worked in brothels in Calais and Boulogne. There was even an old procuress who wanted the young people to join her and sleep with the German troops."

Life at the start was peaceful though strange to young Madeleine because the British women wanted her to join in games and sit on committees. Her closest friend became Sofka Skipworth, the White Russian widow of an English officer.

Soon they were joined by American internees, and then in 1943 strange people arrived with more or less official papers or sometimes just bearing letters from consuls saying that relations abroad would guarantee to support them.

"They had been rounded up just before the Warsaw ghetto was destroyed because the Germans announced that all those who had American or South American papers should come out and they would be sent to camps in other parts of Europe, where they would be exchanged. Very few of them were capable of resisting the temptation.

"The first thing we thought we could do was teach them English to help them when they went abroad. Only the men came to class. It was difficult to get their attention and sometimes they would enter the class through the window instead of the door or leave before it was over. You had the impression that they lived in fear, they couldn't sit still."

If the adults were silent about what they had endured and about what they knew they faced, the children were, as children are, more open. The British nuns in the camp gave them lessons and they made drawings. "That was how we realized what they had been through because they would endlessly draw the same pictures of Nazis shooting kids, throwing people out of the windows."

Gradually there was some mixing with the adults, and Skipworth and White realized there were two ways to help: to inform foreign governments and international organizations of these people's plight and to remember them if all efforts failed. As it turned out, they could only do the latter.

Skipworth, intrepid and well connected, smuggled out lists of the Jews and the countries for which they had papers and wrote to friends and officials.

The letters were not exactly ignored. "They all tried very hard but it was just at the wrong moment because there was D-Day and things were moving. All energies were focused on these things, the leaders all said the only thing we can do for these Jews is win the war. They didn't realize that when the war had been won there would be practically nobody left."

A few official replies offering guarantees came on July 15, 1944, but the Jews had been deported to Auschwitz via Drancy in two convoys, leaving Vittel on April 18 and May 16. A few escaped and were hidden by Skipworth, White and their friends; a few attempted suicide. Skipworth was ordered to sit with the failed suicides in the camp hospital. "What do you say to people half dead whose families had been taken away?"

There were no illusions about what deportation meant. One man on the first convoy threw a note from the train addressed to a Paris friend and it was miraculously delivered. "ATTENTION!" it said. "We have been betrayed and lied to. We are in the train for Auschwitz. Our end is near. Write to Vittel and say that in a few days we will be dead."

Sofia Skipworth and Madeleine White were repatriated to England and, after White returned to France and married, remained in constant touch until Skipworth died in February. Steinberg lives in Paris and gives free English lessons to immigrants. She has been asked for photographs of the Vittel children for a memorial to child deportees. "But there are no photographs, of course," she said.

There are some poems by Itzhak Katzenelson, a Vittel internee who died in Auschwitz and whose eleven-year-old daughter had previously been murdered in Treblinka. They are laments almost unbearable to read:

> *They are no more.*
> *Do not ask anything, anywhere the world over.*
> *All is empty*
> *They are no more.*

There is a plaque in Vittel to the deportees but it does not give their names. As for the camp itself, it is now part of the Club Méditerranée.

June 11, 1994

LETTING LOOSE
AND HOLDING DOWN

PARIS—In the nineteenth century, folk traditions began to be recorded and studied by local notables—teachers, lawyers, notaries—with plenty of time and foolscap at hand. Today, France's rich folklore is a burgeoning subsection of ethnology and holidays that used to offer a larky respite from hard peasant life are being scrutinized for their political and economic ramifications.

Georges Duby's preface to *Fêtes en France* (published by Editions du Chêne) is an example of the new approach. Were the traditional holidays a pretext for merrymaking, pagan jollities connected to farming life? No: they were used by the Establishment to keep the peasants in order. "Purified by the tumult, people return to their places, to calm, order and habit," Mr. Duby writes. No wonder, he says, that local holidays were especially encouraged during the nineteenth century, when country folk became repressed, second-class citizens.

Folk traditions also have an economic side, Mr. Duby says: "Today's world treats ancient holidays as consumer objects." This, of course, has always been true in the literal sense: French fetes seem inevitably to be connected with the consumption of food and drink. One Mardi Gras fete in the Pyrenees, La Fête à l'Ours, positively requires that participants be well oiled before the fun begins.

Easter being the most radiant and hopeful of holidays, it is also, after Lenten sacrifices, a superb time for eating. As Robert de Sorbon, confessor of St. Louis and founder of the Sorbonne in 1253, put it: "Today, the sermon will be short but the table long. One must celebrate the end of Lent."

"Families awaited the great day with agitation, and housewives would bustle around preparing the dishes," G. Bidault de l'Isle, a genial collector of folklore of the old school, has written.

Sometimes they couldn't wait. A collective vision of a huge cake and bottles of wine once interrupted an Easter sermon in the Yonne, and in Semur a table loaded with wine bottles would be set up in the nave as a sign of the joys that would follow Communion.

In parts of Burgundy the traditional Easter dish was ham, especially *jambon persillé*. Lamb was preferred in the Vendée, while the Jura and Poitou celebrated with game *pâté*. The north, fed up with eating salted fish all through Lent, welcomed Easter as "saltless Sunday" and celebrated by eating fresh meat all day long. In Alsace, engaged couples would share a pretzel as a pledge of eternal love.

In many parts of France bacon omelette was a traditional Easter dish. Eggs laid on Good Friday were kept as long as possible because their virtues would ward off illness (in the Côte d'Or lentils eaten on Good Friday erased one's sins).

According to tradition, one was not to work on Good Friday, and on that day ships flew their flags at half mast. However, if one put out one's flea-ridden sheets before dawn on Good Friday, the fleas would flee. Or better still, and more typically French, if you leave your dishcloth in the sink during Holy Week, the fleas will jump over to your neighbor's house.

In the Côte d'Or, if the laundry was soaked before sunrise on Good Friday, it would help preserve a child's health and also cure worms. In the Nièvre a pilgrimage to the Fontaine des Bitoux on Easter Monday, combined with a rinsing of the eyes in the fountain's water, provided a nice outing and protected one's vision, while a visit to the Fontaine Saint-Georges in the Côte d'Or would clear up ear troubles.

Along with food and health, Easter provides for a third French obsession, romance. On Easter Monday, the young girls of Sens would go to the Fontaine d'Azon to learn about their marriage prospects. Each girl would set a pin in the water and hold her breath. If the pin floated, she was sure to be a bride within the year. If it sank, she lost not only her pin but her hopes until the following year, when she could try again.

If Easter in France sounds good enough to celebrate twice a year, that, too, can be done. In 841, the sons of Louis le Débonnaire delivered Fontenoy in the Yonne to him, and the battle went down in history as having taken place on Easter. The locals, thinking the battle had taken place in September, assumed Easter fell in September and traditionally celebrated it then.

In fact, the battle did not take place on Easter. Nor did it take place in September. It seems to have been fought in June, but nobody cares. September is a nicer month for Easter than June because June is too close to Easter.

March 25, 1978

BE CAREFUL,
IT'S MUSHROOM SEASON AGAIN

PARIS—Diderot wrote in the *Encyclopédie* that mushrooms should be sent back to the dung heap where they are born, but he was a rare Frenchman. When the wild mushroom season opens here, the temptation to show off one's knowledge and to acquire something for free is irresistible, and sometimes fatal.

"Each year there are deaths but the press doesn't talk about them anymore," a member of the Société Mycologique de France said at last Sunday's annual mushroom salon, which, suitably, is held at the Faculty of Pharmacy and attracts more visitors per square inch than the Cézanne exhibition at the Grand Palais.

The Mushroom Society has 1,800 members and in addition to the salon organizes weekend mushroom walks in the Paris region. No longer can the *Ungulina inzengae* be found on the Ile Saint

Louis and specimens growing in the Tuileries are usually trampled beyond recognition, but one member said he finds plenty of mushrooms in the Luxembourg Gardens—"mycologically interesting," he added, "but not for the frying pan."

At the salon hundreds of varieties collected by members were displayed on paper plates on which colored napkins had been laid to indicate whether the mushroom was to be eaten (green), to be thrown out (yellow) or avoided (red). Warnings abounded: "Careful! Possible Confusion," "All Truly Toxic Mushrooms Have an Excellent Taste." The biggest crowd was around the *Boletus*—the celebrated *cèpe,* only three varieties of which are toxic.

Names are no help: the Death Trumpet is perfectly safe and the false *girolle* is better to eat than the true *girolle,* which smells of apricots. The Inky Black is edible but provokes congestion, humming in the ears and reddening of the face if the eater touches wine or hard liquor the same day.

Amateur mycologists trust to their noses as well as their eyes although to the uninitiated the predominant smell is of old socks. It isn't easy since one expert has listed 275 identifiable odors: one mushroom is described as smelling of flour, another of rancid flour; another smells of caterpillars and yet another of old candle grease. *Amanita citrina* smells of raw potatoes, the lethal *Amanita phalloides* smells sweetly of old roses.

The Amanita family is among the trickiest: *Amanita caesarea* is considered one of the finest eating mushrooms but may have got its name when Agrippina served them to the Emperor Claudius, mixing in a few *Amanita phalloides* in a successful attempt to put Nero on the throne.

Amanita phalloides, the death cap mushroom, accounts for more than 90 percent of fatalities and, in addition to being pleasantly fragrant, is particularly handsome, with a cap in subtle Armani khaki-gray and a fresh creamy underside. A lethal dose for a man weighing eighty kilograms is fifty grams, according to Jean

Bourdelle's *Les Champignons,* and death may occur within twenty-four hours. By contrast, *Cortinarius orellanus* takes several months to kill and a massive dose of three hundred grams is required to do the deed.

Wild mushrooms may be an efficient way of unloading an unwanted mother-in-law—"The Murderer Awaits in the Woods," an old newspaper headline once read—but the chief attraction of mushroom picking, according to one member of the mycological society, is that they are free. Legislation on mushroom picking is disturbingly vague: Article 547 of the Civil Code states that the fruits of the earth belong to the person who owns it but a ministerial directive of 1979 advises landowners to be tolerant of intruders.

In the south of France, where passion is notoriously unbridled, and where in addition to the *cèpe* the delicious *sanguin* is an autumn joy, mushroom violence is an annual event. "Aggressed by Mushroom Hunters" ran a recent headline in *Nice-Matin,* telling how a landowner in the Var had been beaten up on his own property, which then led to a municipal ruling that mushroom pickers must leave an identity card and car number at the police station before setting off on their hunt. Farther east, in the Mercantour area of the Alpes-Maritimes, there used to be annual warnings about Italians who crossed the border—sometimes by taxi—to pick mushrooms that are rightfully French. Now the situation has degenerated to the point where even decent French citizens transgress and the tiny village of Moulinet has regretfully been obliged to take strong measures against mushroom rustlers.

Residents of Moulinet may continue to forage at will but non-residents must buy a permit for one hundred francs and foreigners must pay four hundred francs. "Our aim is to eradicate professional mushroom thieves, some of whom come armed with rakes," the assistant mayor told *Nice-Matin.*

Mushroom police now patrol the area and arrest those whose baskets or plastic bags contain more than the authorized maximum of five kilograms. Gendarmes so far have seized two perpetrators each carrying ten kilograms of *sanguins,* which cost about 140 francs a kilo on the market. They were each fined 75 francs on the spot and, *pour l'exemple,* were obliged to watch while their prize was reduced to dust before their very eyes.

October 7, 1995

MONSIEUR LE PERPETUEL
TO THE RESCUE OF ENGLISH

PARIS—Why not an English Academy, created along the lines of the Académie Française, to protect the language against Americanisms? The idea has been put forward in an English magazine, *The Author*, by Maurice Druon, writer, former minister of culture and, since 1986, Perpetual Secretary of the Académie Française.

France having lost the battle when the Toubon law to purge the French language of foreign invasions dissolved into one big hoot, Druon is calling on Britain to stem the tide of what he terms the dark side of Amerenglish, "which flows through the audiovisual media, the publicity and travel businesses, banks, laboratories and modern industries, a jumble of abbreviations, quasi-phonetically simplified spellings, slapdash neologisms, botched etymology, grammar disregarded, vulgarity promoted."

His rescue attempt comes none too soon, Druon said in his

office, which is lined with seventeenth- and early-eighteenth-century portraits of academicians squarely facing immortality. English is already more severely corrupted than French: in fifty years at most, he warns, a dictionary may be needed for the English and Americans to understand each other.

"It may be that one notices it less because English syntax is less precise than French. Dare I say that English is the language that is easiest to speak badly, which is one reason for its success. French is too difficult—one always feels one is making a mistake."

One does, and usually one is. Indeed, the highest compliment one can pay a Frenchman is to say that he speaks good French. This was always said of de Gaulle, even by his opponents, and apparently one of the many disturbing things about the National Front leader, Jean-Marie Le Pen, is his mastery of the past subjunctive.

"One cannot say better of a Frenchman than that he speaks good French," Druon said. "It is the Academy that is responsible for this attitude toward language and that confers class to a style of speech.

"In England if you hear a public speaker who mumbles you can be sure he is a Conservative or perhaps a lord. If he speaks a careful English he is probably Labor. In France it is different."

While in France language is style, in Britain, Druon observes, it is not done to be brilliant. "If you have been well brought up you must not appear too clever." In France a writer is honored as an *homme de lettres*. "In England everyone writes and says it's just a hobby."

French became the official language of France in 1539; the academy was founded by Cardinal de Richelieu in 1635. "We are certainly the country where language is an affair of state. The Academy has the status of a higher court."

But can one legislate language? "No more than the Church can legislate morals," Drouon replied. "It can give a sense of sin. That is our role, to give a sense of sin."

Ruddy, spiffy and effulgent, Druon came to know Britain with the Free French during World War II. He speaks English but clearly delights in orotund French. "To speak English is a necessity; to speak French is a privilege."

As an anglophile, why does he want the British to look as silly as France did during the Toubon ban on linguistic contaminants? He says the official attempt to ban Americanisms was good for two reasons: instructions for machinery and appliances should, for safety's sake, be in the user's language and not in computerized American, and so should labor contracts. "Apart from that, I don't see why in golf a bunker should be called an *obstacle de sable* and a birdie a *oiselet*. In that case, ban the use of the word *golf*, too."

As Perpetual Secretary Druon is dedicated to the prestige of the academy and enforces de Gaulle's ruling that, in terms of protocol, academicians rank just below cabinet ministers (although in order to benefit they must appear in the academician's uniform, which is very hot). The academy is the essence of France's notion of its civilizing mission in the world: it was Druon who welcomed the American astronauts after their moon flight "in the name of civilization," causing a giggle or two.

"We are the court of appeal—is a phrase French?—a sort of moral magistrature. To speak well implies certain moral and physical standards."

While proposing that the British found their own academy, Druon admits that this is unlikely to happen since the English lack the special relationship with their own language that the French have. A club might be more in character, he thinks. "After all, some clubs were founded as the direct result of a particular historical or political circumstance. It was the Reform Bill that gave rise to the Reform Club," he wrote in *The Author.*

Of course the odd thing about the Académie Française is that this most French institution could have been invented by Lewis Carroll. Druon agrees that it is mighty eccentric.

Academicians wear a uniform called the *habit vert,* which is usually black. They write a dictionary every half century and then start again. They are inaccurately called immortal and their secretary, Druon, is known as *le Perpetuel*.

"Among the Immortals I am the Perpetual," Druon said, "I call myself a walking pleonasm." He is formally addressed as *Monsieur le Secrétaire Perpetuel*. "Even though we say *tu* to each other, I am Monsieur le Secrétaire Perpetuel or more familiarly Monsieur le Perpetuel. That is the height of familiarity."

He is the academy's thirtieth perpetual secretary, the first being Valentin Conrart, whom Richelieu appointed even though he was a Protestant. "Continuity is the main thing," Druon said. "Richelieu said there would be only one perpetual secretary, Valentin Conrart, who stayed at the post for forty-one years. There have been other names since—the thirtieth name is mine—but the post remains unchanged.

"The word *immortality* does not mean the immortality of the academicians, it is the immortality of the language."

In its ability to perpetuate itself the French Academy is not unlike the House of Lords, Druon says. "And some of the academicians act as strangely as lords," he adds. A group portrait in Druon's office painted to celebrate the three hundredth birthday of the academy suggests what an odd mix it has always been. Among the Immortals then were Henri Bergson, Marshal Pétain, Paul Valéry and François Mauriac.

The academy may be the epitome of the Establishment but, says Druon, "it is an Establishment that is not an Establishment. There is not one of us who has not at some moment of his life acted against the accepted rules of his milieu. We are almost all exceptions, that is why we are here.

"All Academicians have something exceptional about them," he added. "In some cases it's luck."

July 15, 1995

WHY A LEOPARD
CANNOT CHANGE ITS SPOTS

PARIS—No one in France could be Formerly Known as Prince or, as in England, change his name by deed poll to Screaming Lord Sutch. Nor could he craftily change his name to Chirac or Mitterrand. As the historian Richard Cobb once observed, the French are less citizens of their country than the creatures of its administration, and the administration rules on everything down to what name a person is allowed to have.

The rules on name changing are partly a matter of national pride—it has been estimated that by the twelfth century 90 percent of the inhabitants of the southern regions had surnames, well in advance of most of France's neighbors—and partly the administration's distrust of the administrated. In a definitive article on the subject, a member of the Conseil d'Etat, the final arbiter on the subject, notes that the changing of a name affects not only the individual but *la patrie:*

"It is to the public interest that certain family names not disappear and that people be unable to use a name to hide their true identity," Daniel Pepy wrote in *Les Changements du Nom dans le Droit Français,* published in 1967.

But even for the administration times are changing. In one of the few modifications since the basic law on surnames was passed during the revolution, in 1985 women were allowed to join their maiden names to their husbands' and the recent flow of immigrants has increased the demand for new names to which the administration can only accede for fear of computer and employee breakdowns when dealing with a name like Vissitthiedeth, Camatchysiudirame, or Trab Vinhn Tan Tan Gapegassam, to say nothing of the alarming shortage of vowels in Szczpkowsk and Wryszcz.

So considerable has been the population change that the archetypal French name Dupont no longer is, according to Jean-Louis Beaucarnot's study, *Vous et Votre Nom,* published by Laffont in 1992. These days in France there are more Garcias than Duponts and only two hundred more people named Dupont than Martinez. On the other hand, while a stringent study in 1989 showed that there are only 3,225 noble families in France, there are 15,000 that have contrived to sound noble.

The most common name in France, says Beaucarnot, is Michel Martin. He has found fifty-eight in Paris alone, three of whom live on the same street. He has also found six thousand Barres, several of them called Raymond like the former prime minister, and it would be no problem to invite an Alain Delon, a Jean-Jacques Rousseau, a Proust or Pétain to dinner, to say nothing of Monsieur Henri Quatre.

Those who want to change their names have to have a great deal of patience and at least four thousand francs to cover expenses. The first step is an application to the Ministry of Justice giving reasons for the request, then the publication of the request in the *Journal Officiel* as well as in a newspaper located near the applicant's domicile. Then the Conseil d'Etat rules, the change if accepted is again printed in the *Journal Officiel* and will be effective in a year's time, the whole process having taken about three years.

No one, according to jurisprudence, should be obliged to bear a name that is too foreign or sounds too silly. But what is silly? Canard, Vache and Veau have been deemed worthy of change, while Boeuf, Taureau and Chèvre were rejected. Monsieur Léopard could not change his spots but Monsieur Chameau (camel) lost his hump. Monsieur Moche was accepted while Monsieur Vilain was turned down, although both names mean ugly.

The son of a murderer or a rapist can change his name, the son of a mere bank robber cannot. There are 214 people named Cochon (pig) who have changed and 900 who have not. Often people who live in the country and are aware of the rural roots of their otherwise embarrassing names have no wish to change—Bordel, for example, originally meant an isolated farm—and an Alsatian named Hittler didn't even understand Beaucarnot's question about a change.

"Adolf, so what?" he replied. "I have nothing to do with him and everyone here in the Bas-Rhin knows it."

One group who have been encouraged to change their names are Jews, the theory being that fewer Jewish names will avoid "a repetition of the events of the last war," according to Daniel Pepy. "The Conseil d'Etat is ready to look favorably upon any request if they estimate, fear or suspect a Jewish consonance."

But again times have changed since Pepy's article and today there are Jews who wish to resume their ancestral names. The request is not always accepted because the court cannot comprehend why anyone would willingly give up the generous gift of a truly French name. One man cited by Beaucarnot had such prob-

lems trying to take back the Jewish name that his father had changed in 1940 that he went for psychiatric aid to Jacques Lacan in a failed attempt to solve his identity crisis. Fortunately, the man was a playwright who adopted his former name as a nom de plume, which was eventually legitimized.

The importance of a name cannot be overemphasized. "I shall inhabit my name," said the poet St. Jean Perse, born Alexis Léger. Nor can its spelling: the two rrs in Mitterrand were deemed suspicious in their excess by one expert.

The names that bring their bearers the most grief are those with scatological or sexual connotations, though here again times change. It is hard to know whether Monsieur Abdelazzia, who in 1955 changed his name to Gay, would today be happy or sad.

One of the most troublesome names is Cocu (cuckold) and its variants. So many people have this name that Beaucarnot includes a map of France showing where it can be found, which is almost everywhere. Those wishing to change it are likely to find a friendly ear.

Attitudes toward one's name can indicate narcissism, a castration complex, phantom identity problems and incestuous tendencies, Beaucarnot writes, as well as the simple fear of raising a giggle every time one is introduced.

Not surprisingly in the 1960s a Monsieur Cocu and Monsieur Meurdesoif (Mr. Dying-for-a-Drink) founded an association, the Defense of the Patronymically Handicapped. It went well at first, then gradually shrank as members found more satisfying names. It finally died out completely when M. Meurdesoif changed his name to Meuroy.

July 27, 1996

WORDS & IMAGES

A VINTAGE YEAR FOR DURAS

PARIS—In some forty years as a *femme de lettres,* Marguerite Duras has achieved a rare immortality: She has become an adjective. What *durassien* means depends on which side you are on. She arouses fascination, irritation, adulation, boredom—sometimes all at once. Her prose is difficult, spare, obsessive, easy enough to parody and very hard to imitate. She makes bad habits such as one-word sentences work. Always. And in both subject matter and in her actual phrasing, she repeats herself, often.

"Robbe-Grillet said, 'She repeats. She says again things that she has already said,'" Duras remarked in the theater where she is directing a revised version of her play, *La Musica.*

"He confuses things, Robbe-Grillet. He thinks that to repeat means to say the same thing. But if you say things in another way, they are new. He didn't say that maliciously," she added. "Easily perhaps, but not maliciously."

La Musica, which opened in Paris this week and which Duras also refers to as *Musica Musica* and *Musica II,* began in 1966 as a one-act play for British television in which a just-divorced young couple meet at a hotel in Evreux for the last time. A new act has them talking in the hotel room without stop until dawn. "I make them talk for hours and hours," Duras said. "Just for the sake of talking."

Hours of talk is definitely *durassien* and, especially in her films, it drives some people mad (her film *Le Camion* was a monologue by Duras with an occasional reverse shot of Gérard Depardieu). It is a peculiarly French phenomenon for respected writers—Cocteau, Malraux, Robbe-Grillet—to direct films, but none has been as un-remitting as Duras.

With over a dozen films to her credit, she is an active and often innovative filmmaker. *Cahiers de Cinema* devoted a special issue to her in 1980 in which she gave a very funny account of filming with Godard and qualified her film *Aurélia Steiner* as one of the most important pictures ever made.

Her pictures are so static and unvisual, says one French critic, that one suspects that she makes films in order to destroy the cinema. It isn't a medium she seems to love: In yet another book of homage she is quoted as saying, "I make films to fill my time. If I had the strength to do nothing, I would do nothing."

Talking in the theater after a rehearsal of *La Musica,* she says she makes films between books in order to keep writing. To write, she has said, is to be unable not to write. She is extremely productive and even a severe bout of alcoholism did not stop her from writing: "When I am writing I am not dying."

Next month she will come out with a book of four pieces about the Occupation. (She lived then, as she does now, on rue Saint Benoit in Saint-Germain-des-Prés, and saved the life of a fellow Resistance member called Morland, real name François Mitterrand.)

The publication of the new book will mark the end of a most remarkable Duras season in which, in addition to *Musica* and a film,

Les Enfants, she came out with a novel, *L'Amant* (The Lover), which became a best-seller even before Duras talked about it on France's best television program, Bernard Pivot's *Apostrophes,* and which went on to win the prestigious Goncourt literary prize.

L'Amant is set in Indochina, a French colony when Duras was born there in 1914. Her widowed mother (her father had been a math teacher) taught at a mixed-race school, a demeaning position for a Frenchwoman at the time, and scrabbled hard to raise her daughter and two sons.

L'Amant reexplores the period Duras described in *Un Barrage contre le Pacifique* (1950), but she says that while her family was still alive she wrote around, rather than about, them. If some of the material in the new book is familiar, the story is not.

"The story of my life does not exist," Duras writes in *L'Amant.* "It does not exist. There is never a center. No road, no line." A critic in *Le Monde* crossly noted, "Duras says the story of my life does not exist. This is clearly untrue. She never stops telling it to us."

The three Donnadieu children (she became Duras when she became a writer) grew up like proud and unruly savages. At the age of fifteen and a half Marguerite takes her first lover, a Chinese twelve years her senior, takes him for her own pleasure, which is immense, and for his fortune, which is considerable. The affair ends a year and a half later, when the girl (the book is written in the first and third persons) leaves for France. "The book doesn't really end," Duras said. "At its close it is just beginning. *L'Amant* is like a book that is opening, a possibility. That's why people threw themselves on it."

L'Amant is indeed an extraordinary book, *durassien* but totally accessible. It was written mostly at Neauphle-le-Château, a village near Paris whose other distinguished residents include Deanna Durbin and, until he returned in triumph to Iran, Ayatollah Ruhollah Khomeini. While Duras can labor over a short text for a year, she breezed through *L'Amant* in three months.

"Sometimes I worked ten hours a day. But without fatigue.

People have asked me why it's such a success and I think it is because I found a great happiness in writing it, a great happiness that is transmitted to the reader.

"That's a new phenomenon in French book-selling, because to be serious you had to bore people. I didn't do it purposely, but the book doesn't bore.

"It's a difficult book but I think people understand that I didn't make it difficult on purpose."

With the publication of *L'Amant,* photographs of the young Duras were given to the press: a most arresting face, quite lovely and untrustworthy, with the impenitent eyes of a child guerrilla or a subway pickpocket. *L'Amant* was first intended as a collection of old pictures, rather than a novel, but it became centered on a photograph that was never taken, what Duras calls the absolute photograph: Marguerite, aged fifteen and a half, stands on a ferry over the Mekong River wearing a man's pink fedora with a black hatband, a pale silk dress so worn it is nearly transparent and gold dancing shoes. On the river bank a young Chinese watches her from his long, black, chauffeur-driven car.

He is the lover but there are other implied desires—for the girl's schoolmate, Hélène Lagonelle, and above all for her two brothers: the sweet, slow younger one whose body resembles that of her lover, and the dangerous and bad older brother who robs her in Paris during the Occupation when her husband is in a German camp and who reminds her of the Robert Mitchum character in *The Night of the Hunter,* a film that makes one faint with horror, she says. She has seen it four times.

One senses that what pleases her most in *L'Amant* is her liberation in having talked freely about her family without naming culprits. "There are no villains. Everyone is innocent, even my older brother."

Because *L'Amant* began as a photo album, Duras says she said to herself that she would pay less attention to her writing than usual. From this she accidentally developed a style she calls *écrit-*

ure courante, a cursive style that she describes as "writing abandoned to itself, left to itself. I sometimes had the feeling that the writing was going faster than I was."

Duras is a small terrier of a woman. Although she feels that critics ignored her over the last ten years, she has staunch admirers, and Paul Webster and Nicholas Powell, in their recent book, *St.-Germain-des-Prés,* call her the queen of the quarter. She talks much as she writes: the pauses, the repetitions, the sudden rhythms all demand attention. They are the verbal equivalent of the Ancient Mariner's grasp. There are lots of stories, some perhaps true, about Duras groupies; one feels she does not discourage them.

"My readers, who were already fanatical about me, were cross about the Prix Goncourt. They said they are taking you away from us, you belonged only to us."

She belongs to no one and still considers herself a Créole, a French woman born outside France. "All my books come from that. I am very glad to be born elsewhere."

Of her books she prefers *Le Ravissement de Lol V. Stein* (1964) and *Le Vice-consul* (1965). "I am very happy when I read *Lol V. Stein* but the strongest and most violent joy is *Le Vice-consul.* I think there aren't many books like it in our century. I'm not being pretentious. I have a certain idea of myself," she added, smiling. "One can call it pretentious, I don't care. It's what I think."

A former member of the French Communist party, she is no longer politically active and no longer claims an interest in feminism ("I discussed it politely in newspapers for years but in fact I never gave it a thought."). After neglect and alcoholism (her cure, typically, was documented in a book by an admirer) she is on top right now and enjoying it. She was quite pleased to tell the astonished Pivot on television that Sartre was not a writer and did not know what writing is.

"Sartre," she said in the theater after the rehearsal, "is one reason why the French are mentally and politically retarded. He considered himself *the* interpreter of Marxism. You know how in religion you haven't the right to go directly to God, you must go by way of a saint? Well Sartre and Sartrism were the great intercessors of Marxism. No, he wasn't a writer. He wasn't."

With a grin that, despite her years and distinctions, can only be called cheeky, she adds that suddenly she finds it easier to talk frankly—about her family, about the Resistance, about Sartre. "It's all the same to me now, I couldn't care less. Getting old has its good points, too, I assure you. You'll see."

May 22, 1985

SIMONE DE BEAUVOIR TALKS,
AND TALKS

*... self knowledge is impossible
and the best one can hope for
is self-revelation.*

SIMONE DE BEAUVOIR,
THE PRIME OF LIFE, 1960

PARIS—Over the years Simone de Beauvoir has revealed herself in part in four volumes of memoirs and in books of reflections on old age and death. Photographs of her handsome, turbaned head have been seen across the world, she has spoken openly of her relations with Jean-Paul Sartre and others, such sobriquets as the Beaver and La Grande Sartreuse are familiar to all. Yet she remains remote: the form of self-revelation she has chosen is also deeply self-protective. She is lengthily, and proudly, self-critical, to the point where self-criticism can be taken for self-praise.

Last spring, at the age of seventy, Simone de Beauvoir was filmed talking to nine friends, including Sartre. The 110-minute film, *Simone de Beauvoir,* directed by Josée Dayan, opened this week in three Paris movie houses. It starts with Simone de Beauvoir telling the writer Claude Lanzmann why she agreed to make the film:

"One could say vanity, because I want people to know me: there are many people who haven't read me and will know me through this film. One could also say from a desire for recognition, because among those who have read me there are many who are mistaken about me. Those who have not read me are often also mistaken. This film is a way of setting things straight but the two go together—vanity and a desire to speak the truth. . . .

"There may be people who will dislike me even more after having seen me. But it seems to me that it will give a more correct picture than the one drawn not only from my books but from the reputation certain critics and journalists have given me."

The result, since Simone de Beauvoir chose both her interlocutors and the subjects they would discuss, is rather like a French intellectual's version of *This Is Your Life:* as discomfiting as the original but lacking its spontaneity.

The film, which is beautifully assembled, came about by chance. Josée Dayan and her collaborator, the actress Malka Ribowska, had been making a TV film on Wagner in Venice and thought of making Beauvoir's *La Femme Rompue* their next project. They wrote unsuccessfully to Simone de Beauvoir, whose work had never been filmed, then returned to Venice for retakes.

"One day I saw Sartre and Simone de Beauvoir at Florian in the Piazza San Marco," Malka Ribowska says. "I was wearing my Cosima Wagner costume and couldn't approach them, but I told Josée who went racing over."

Surprised, Beauvoir agreed to meet the two in Paris and ultimately to write the dialogue for *La Femme Rompue,* which was a success on French TV. "She was very moved by the film; she said she was more touched by the character as played by Malka than by the heroine in the book," Josée Dayan says.

From this, Simone de Beauvoir agreed to the documentary, for which she was paid an unspecified sum and which was filmed in ten eight-hour days, in her apartment and in Sartre's. "Imagine

the lucidity—to be able to talk from twelve to eight without flag-
ging," Malka Ribowska says.

Talk she does, in rapid, grating tones, with the air of a lady pri-
oress who is subject to novicelike blushes and hints of tears. The
scenes with Sartre, with whom she has shared nearly fifty years,
are most touching in their formal intimacy (they address each
other as *vous*), although not especially revealing (they include at
least two segments already familiar from Beauvoir's published
memoirs). While Beauvoir remains expectedly humorless, Sartre
is slightly a tease, referring to her at one point as a *dame,* rather
than a *femme, de lettres* and getting a predictable rise.

Of this secretive if talkative woman's personality, little emerges.
She confesses that she can be brutal and abrupt, and at the beginning proves hilariously insensitive when she asks Claude Lanzmann, a former lover, what he thought of her.

"When?" he asks desperately, fencing for time. "At first, or
later?" "At first *and* later," she implacably replies. Lanzmann finally asks the camera to stop.

The picture of remoteness is enforced and legitimized: speaking of the causes in which she has been involved, Simone de
Beauvoir says, "I gave them support but not very much action because I am, after all, an intellectual."

An intellectual indeed, and, with Sartre, the last example in
the West of the intellectual as an international celebrity, as the
images of "existentialist" Saint-Germain-des-Prés and of meetings with heads of state suggest. It is hard to measure Simone de
Beauvoir's eventual place in French literature: possibly she will
endure as the representative and chronicler of that murky and
deeply important period, *l'après-guerre,* most remembered for her
picture of French intellectuals at the Liberation in *The Man-
darins* and for her 1949 book, *The Second Sex.*

The Second Sex, she explains in the film, came about not because she was a feminist but because she felt, typically, that if she

were to continue to write fiction and to begin her own memoirs, she must first make a theoretical study of what it is to be a woman. She only became a feminist fairly recently, long after the book's adoption by the women's movement.

Her intention in writing, Simone de Beauvoir says in the film, has been to speak of her experiences in the hope that they might help others, and to fix these experiences in eternity. She has often written of her lifelong fear of death, but says that this is now past.

Her fear may have passed simply because the old are, mercifully, less frightened by death than the middle-aged and the young, or it may have passed because, as she says, she reasoned herself out of her anguish and rage: "I cannot be angry at God, in whom I do not believe, I cannot be angry at my cells and my body, which are those of a person of my age. So I have no reason to be enraged."

What she finds unbearable now is the prospect of the death of those close to her: "The death of certain people would deal me a blow that, if not mortal, would make me lose all taste for life." (At the start of her liaison with Sartre, she wrote, "I knew no harm could ever come to me from him—unless he were to die before I did.")

Having written so much about her life, its events are no longer very warm and alive to her, Simone de Beauvoir says. There is little trace of the exalted young woman who lived, as she has said, in a condition of Kantian optimism, where you *ought* implies you *can*. Instead, she is resigned.

She used to see life in terms of thunder or light, never gray, she says. "Now it is no longer light and dark, but gray—often a rose-tinted gray because I still have much pleasure and happiness, but no longer the ups and downs between happiness and despair. One might say that I subside."

January 4, 1979

Simone de Beauvoir died in 1986, six years after Sartre, on whose corpse she had thrown herself in the hospital.

V.S. PRITCHETT'S
CHEERFUL LAMENTS

LONDON—The word people most often use about V.S. Pritchett is one that is almost never applied to writers: nice. Moreover, it is true.

"I'm rather talkative. People always think you're nice if you talk to them," he says. "I don't get involved in quarrels with people because I find them so interesting in themselves. I don't think I'm nice. I'm a person of good will and I get along with people."

Now in his eightieth year, Pritchett is a nimble and responsive talker, a discreetly snappy dresser with the anonymous look of a successful professional man. His face, he dispassionately insists, is a pudding. "I've got no bones and a squashed little nose." Every day in his house near Regent's Park he lays a pastry board across his knees, and writes.

On the Edge of the Cliff, his latest collection of short stories, is just out in the United States and will be published in London in the new year. He is one of the finest practitioners of the dying art of the short story—dying, he says, because there are so few literary magazines left and because "I don't know if people do it now with the same conviction that it is a form itself."

Although he has written novels he says he lacks the novelist's vegetative temperament: he sees the short story as a protest against the discursive. Because form is decisive, the short story is closest to poetry.

"You're used to using images, a lot of short stories are really like sonnets or lyrical poems. Browning is my idea of a good short-story writer and a good poet."

Like poetry, short-story writing can be financially unrewarding. Pritchett has taught in American universities—"teaching them to unwrite what they had done, making them unwrite their sentences"—and for thirty years he wrote weekly literary essays. He is, says Gore Vidal, no mean critic himself, "the best English-language critic of—well, the *living* novel." Pritchett resents the time he has had to devote to reviewing: "for myself—if not for the reader—one or two good short stories are worth all the criticism in the world," he has said. He has also said, "In my criticism, even more than my stories, I am self-portrayed."

"I've been told this and probably thought it was so," he says today. "You're apt to lean perhaps not on your experiences, but the results of your experiences.

"I read in order to learn how to write. The scholarly critic is interested not in readers but in the library point of view. I'm rather like the traditional periodical writer—Hazlitt, Goldsmith or for that matter Virginia Woolf, who wrote for the common reader, by which she meant the educated reader."

It was a triumph for Pritchett to become a writer at all. Born in lodgings over a toy shop in Ipswich, the son of an improvident salesman father "with the bumptiousness of a god" and a mother he describes as "a rootless London pagan, a fog-worshipper," he had, by the age of twelve, changed houses fourteen or eighteen times depending on who was counting.

At twenty, having spent four years working at a leather factor's near the London docks, he put on a pair of classy red shoes—the latest color, bought wholesale in the trade—and went to Paris, where he worked for a photographer and sold glue, shellac, ostrich feathers and theater tickets.

It was the riotous 1920s but Pritchett was earning a living, not sitting in cafés. "When I read memoirs about the Paris of the Steins, Sylvia Beach, Joyce, Hemingway and Scott Fitzgerald, I am cast down," he wrote in his autobiography. "I was there. I may have passed them in the street. I simply had never heard of them."

He bought *Ulysses* but didn't read it for several years. Later, when he returned to London he was told that as an aspiring writer he should move to a place called Bloomsbury. Consulting a map, he found he already lived there.

His first published work was a joke printed in this newspaper and never paid for. Since he wanted to write he became a roving journalist, a profession to which he says he was totally unsuited as he has no nose for news and is the enemy of truth. "If I'd gone to see someone I should have put down what he said. Instead, I would put down what he didn't say or should have said."

Travel brought not only freedom but the discipline of trying to observe strangers and understand them. Spain, where he went after France and Ireland, was the most demanding and so the most rewarding. The strangeness of Spain, he has written, was evident from the moment he crossed the border at Hendaye: "Through France people were as rosy as lawyers and almost buttered. Here they looked corpse-like."

Victor Sawdon Pritchett became V.S. Pritchett professionally because initials were a convention at the time and because, he has said, "to have added the 't' of Victor to a name that already had three, and was made more fidgety by a crush of consonants and two short vowels, seemed ridiculous."

He was knighted in 1975 and still finds it disturbing. "To be referred to as Sir Victor—people don't realize that's the same person as V.S. Pritchett. Bad for trade, as Osbert Sitwell said, bad for trade."

His stories, he once wrote, are mostly laments: a strange word for works of such humor and edgy control. "My brothers and sister and I became skeptical early on, disabused," he says. "We didn't believe in any of the big words. But it's a cheerful lament, a sort of cheerfulness in woe."

His endlessly demanding and dramatizing parents were a burden and still are in memory for, as he wrote in an essay on Pasternak, Pritchett sees memory "not as a fixed picture but as a force in motion, perhaps like a storm that has passed but is still banked up and reverberating."

The pressure of such a family creates a dream life that is good for a writer, he says, and a desire for physical escape: "If you're English you're dying to get away because the place is so small. The wretched British Empire is the result of people wanting to get out.

"Pressure also creates obsessions and I think obsessions are good for a writer. Without an obsession I might have been a bookish chap lazing my life away. England at the time of my boyhood was full of lazy readers—the accountant read Tolstoy, the local councillor was a classical scholar. I might have become the head clerk in a firm who went home nights and read books and didn't talk to his wife."

Thanks also to his family background he produced, with *A Cab at the Door* and *Midnight Oil*, a marvelous autobiography, happily free, like his conversation, of literary anecdotes and reminiscence.

"Some people like reminiscence for its own sake," he says. "I can't bear it. I didn't want to write about my career, I hate careers. I have a bad memory, a fictive memory. If I had told anecdotes I would have made a mess of them if they were true or exaggerated them into the wildest lies. Also, I didn't want to hurt people who are still living."

In *Midnight Oil,* Pritchett writes, "I see myself as a practicing writer who gives himself to a book as he gives himself to any human experience." With each new piece of writing, he says, "I have to make that terrifying bridge with my real life and learn to write again." Facing the blank page becomes harder, not easier.

And if he can't write?

"I write. What you want to write is something that comes out of the habit of writing," he said.

December 8, 1979

ELISABETH LUTYENS:
"A DOG BARKS AND A COMPOSER COMPOSES"

LONDON—Elisabeth Lutyens, who has been called the most radical British composer of her generation, turned seventy-five last summer, an event marked by a handful of concerts and interviews. Interviewers who called her a woman composer did so at their own peril, as a TV talk show host learned.

"I said if he called me a woman composer I'd called him a queer, which he is," Miss Lutyens said. She may be white-haired now and frail, but she is as dauntless and sharp-tongued as she was when she roared at a startled obstetrician while coming out of the anesthetic after the birth of her first child, "And I still want to write music, fuck you!"

But being both a woman and a composer has undoubtedly made her life exceptionally hard. Born to privilege (her father was the architect Sir Edwin Lutyens, her mother the daughter of the

Earl of Lytton), she had two improvident husbands and four children. She supported the family by copying music (her first job was to copy "Limehouse Blues" at ten pence a page) and writing for films and radio. No matter what, she tried to compose a few bars of her own music every day.

"I had a difficult private life," she said dispassionately. "I am fifteen years behind any man. If Britten wrote a bad score they'd say, 'He's had a bad day.' If I'd written one it was because I was a woman."

Feminists who come to her North London house with tracts get as short shrift as those who label her a woman composer.

"Instead of writing useless information about women being abused, why not build a nursery school so women could have two hours a day without Mum, Mum, Mum and quarrel, quarrel, quarrel?

"I am not anti-men, I adore them," Miss Lutyens said. "But I think they're a luxury. Give me a wife any time. Nothing is so cheap as a wife."

Her elegant fingers still wear polish so deep in color that it is almost black but the rheumatoid arthritis that has lately confined her to bed makes ordinary writing impossible and writing music extremely painful. Still, she wrote seven pieces last year: Her output is staggering and she has been accused of being too prolific.

"They want you to write one masterpiece. I have an eighteenth-century view. A dog barks and a composer composes." If a work wasn't played, she says airily, she would just write another. At this point, she says she would scrap it all except a setting of Rimbaud for strings and soprano and a chamber concerto, although she doesn't care much for the concerto form: "To me it's pouring new wine into old bottles."

On her own as a young composer, Elisabeth Lutyens discovered what she later learned was called twelve-tone music. Her commitment to modern music never wavered although in 1930s England it was thought perfectly understandable that a cellist would walk offstage after a few bars of the Webern trio, saying, "I can't play this thing."

There is a certain illogic in people wanting to read the latest books but only to hear the oldest music, she pointed out in her autobiography, *A Goldfish Bowl*. "The average intelligent person is not content to read repeatedly and exclusively the same handful of classics, he acquires new books from libraries and bookshops as they appear. . . . Strangely—to me—the music lover wants just this; the same works from the same classical masters week after repeated week, program after repeated program. And most of the musical powers support and encourage this necrophilia."

She loathed writing her autobiography and only did so in order to record the achievements of her adored second husband, Edward Clark, a conductor who had studied with Schoenberg and was the BBC's chief music planner until he resigned in 1936. He died in 1962.

"He had twenty-three years of unemployment so I know what unemployment is. If you bring a child into the world who may not want to be born, your first responsibility is to the child. I even applied to the Labour Exchange to scrub floors. My husband said, 'I'll conduct or nothing.'"

There is no bitterness. Elisabeth Lutyens may like to rail—"This is a miserable world, it stinks," she says—but she would not complain.

"We're all allowed self-pity for a week after the flu. That's all."

Elisabeth Lutyens developed her considerable verbal gifts while acting as hostess for her father while her mother, Lady Emily, was off on theosophist missions with Krishnamurti. Beautiful and eccentric, Lady Emily was narrowly dissuaded from leading a protest demonstration in the viceregal New Delhi that her husband had designed, and when Elisabeth was wondering how to feed six hungry mouths she sent her a book of household hints: "To air the beds get the third housemaid to sleep in them every third day." Elisabeth dedicated her requiem to her mother but Lady Emily did not attend the performance as she had a dinner party that night.

Sir Edwin was charming, distracted and affectionate. There were five children and it has been said that Sir James Barrie took the Lutyens nursery as his setting for *Peter Pan*.

Not so, says Elisabeth. "Our nursery life was war tooth and nail." In that war she held the uninteresting rank of second youngest and was, her younger sister has written with a suggestion of disapproval, always bent on being different.

She was given violin lessons at the age of nine to cure nail biting and decided to devote herself to music not, she says, from natural talent but from the wish for privacy. Had she gone into the visual arts her father would have been peering over her shoulder, while her mother's family was extremely literary. No one in the family knew anything about music.

She studied in Paris—"France in 1922 was heady," she says—and returned to do battle in England ever after. She disliked what her friend the composer Constant Lambert called the cowpat school of English music. Her work is rigorous and literally inaccessible—rarely played, hardly recorded, even now more readily welcomed by the young than by the Establishment.

A leading British painter praises the asperity of her works; a fashionable conductor admires her intelligence and lineage but finds her music disagreeable. Her friends were more often writers and artists than musicians with such exceptions as Dallapiccola, Virgil Thomson and Stravinsky. "In a few minutes we were banging the table like students," she says of her first meeting with Stravinsky.

The Nobel prize winner Elias Canetti is a friend; Dylan Thomas was an intimate although, as she points out, "So many people say they knew Dylan it's almost more chic not to." She was vivacious company and had smashing legs and fragile health. For a while she was an alcoholic, a condition brought on by having no head for liquor but being obliged to meet BBC producers in pubs to discuss commissions. She is a generous and much appreciated teacher.

Despite the seventy-fifth birthday celebrations, Elisabeth Lutyens says she is still in the wilderness. "Look at this nose," she said. It is impressively long. "I'm an elephant, I never forget but I'm deeply forgiving.

"Everyone says I've got such integrity. That's not a virtue, it's a necessity for an artist. I don't even know what it means."

Her work is changing, she says. For one thing it is getting shorter and she doesn't even like to listen to long-winded composers such as Bruckner anymore. Last year a concert organizer complained that a horn and string quintet she had written lasted only eight minutes.

"If you look at five paintings Turner did of the same subject, the first is lush and naturalistic, the one he did late in life you can hardly see what it is. It's like late Cézanne. I've noticed that with old age—with certain exceptions—people know what to leave out. There is just the skeleton.

"I've got a lot of time to make up. I'm still not beaten," she said. "That's why my bloody body behaving like this annoys me.

"What can a composer do? I'm not as important as a miner. One hopes to have contributed something to the quality of life. I think that's as important as the quantity, don't you?"

January 9, 1982

ERICH SALOMON'S EYE
ON CLEVER HOPES

PARIS—He was, said Aristide Briand, the King of the Indiscreet; another statesman became so used to his presence that he claimed it would be impossible to hold an international conference without him. More recently, he has been called the first of the paparazzi.

Ubiquitous he was, and guileful about taking photographs where it was not allowed. A hollowed-out tome on mathematics allowed him to photograph the gaming rooms at Monte Carlo, a sling over a "broken" arm yielded shots of the U.S. Supreme Court in session, a fedora with a hole proved useful on many occasions. It is perfectly true, says Erich Salomon's son, Peter Hunter Salomon, that his father once used a window washer's ladder to take pictures of an international conference at The Hague; it is, however, untrue that the ladder was held by the secretary of a minister.

But Erich Salomon was far from indiscreet or intrusive. He was ingenious, humorous and, from his photographs, a rather tender man who often seems in complicity with his subjects, which does not prevent him from being sharp and knowing about them. His photographs reflect both the certainty and doubt of the period between the wars. His subjects are confident and powerful, the creators of what Auden called, in "September 1, 1939," the clever hopes of a low dishonest decade.

A small, select Salomon show is now being held in Paris at the Photogalerie. Born in Berlin in 1886, the son of a banker who lost his money in World War I, Erich Salomon tried business and law, then sought to make his fortune with a fleet of chauffeur-driven motorcycles. Unable to find chauffeurs, he took on the job himself, offering this utterly resistible come-on:

"Sit in a sidecar driven by a doctor of law who during the ride will impart inside information on the price of gold and the devaluation of the mark."

Several vicissitudes followed, but by 1931 Salomon was able to celebrate his fifth year in photography in characteristic fashion: he invited four hundred well-known Berliners to a party at the Hotel Kaiserhof, where he showed each guest photographs he had taken of him in secret. They were all delighted.

Salomon took pictures all over Europe and in the United States. A self-portrait shows him in white tie and tails, his camera aiming one way, his eyes another, an anticipatory smile on his lips. His hair stands up in tufts which, according to Tom Hopkinson, the editor of *Picture Post,* rose alarmingly when Salomon was excited.

While Salomon was doing his best work, Hitler's legions were forming, but he didn't photograph the all-too-familiar rigid military parades. He worked in a time now celebrated for its depravity, when his subjects might have been those described by Day Lewis: "The man with his tongue in his cheek, the woman/ with her heart in the wrong place, unhandsome/unwholesome."

But Salomon's pictures show something more significant than

fascism and Berlin decadence: they show the world that made these possible. It is a well-ordered, well-fed, well-dressed, well-behaved world of society lovelies, broad-beamed dowagers, eminent statesmen, international political conferences and small social events such as Elisabeth Schumann singing at an embassy reception to a company that includes the Duchess of Kent, who listens with poised politeness.

Salomon's photographs are about listening, or failing to listen—Stanley Baldwin and Ramsey MacDonald, hands cupped behind their ears, yawning participants at international conferences, public smiles and secret thoughts, conniving heedlessness, the failure to hear or to care.

Very often in group shots one or several people are out of focus, evaporated into their private worlds, and often they are simple poseurs—Alfred Adler carried away by his own eloquence at a psychologists' conference, Aristide Briand jovially pointing out Salomon to a sycophantic group in evening dress.

Sometimes, there is an oblique hint of sinister things to come. A squalid little man in gray socks sits waiting, disturbingly confident, amid the gilded splendor of the Salon de l'Horloge at the Quai d'Orsay. His name is Maurice Privat, and he is the personal astrologer of Pierre Laval.

Salomon was astute enough to move his family to Holland, where his wife had been born, in 1933. But he had, perhaps, too much faith in humanity to go farther, and ten years later he and his wife and son Dirk were deported and in 1944 they died, at Auschwitz.

February 20, 1976

KEEPING BERLIN *BERLINISCH*

BERLIN—Berliners have always had their own view of themselves: not smug in the style of inhabitants of other major cities with monuments and wide boulevards, but the gritty, unruly and sometimes tragically knowing gaze that is a familiar part of Berlin's famous humor and that has always set it attractively apart from the rest of Germany.

Separated not only from the rest of the country but from half of itself, Berlin for many years referred to itself as an island (one of the most popular satirical radio programs of the 1950s was called *Die Insulaner* [The Islanders]). Now it faces becoming whole, becoming the contested capital of the unified Germany, and perhaps becoming no longer uniquely Berlin.

The sense of openness, the optative mood, is thrilling but day-to-day life can be bewildering. If young squatters have easily decamped to cheaper areas (where one squat bears the sign Anarchy and Luxury), middle-aged taxi drivers are uneasy in the East with its unfamiliar streets and vacant lots and unreasonable dead ends, and even the young find East Berliners different in their slang and lack of cheek. "They are foreigners but in a few years we will get together again," sighed a woman taxi driver in a flowered house-dress who had just failed to find one of the East's major streets.

The physical unification of former East and West is in the hands of the Berlin Senate and an advisory council, the Stadtfo-rum, which meets every two weeks to discuss how the city should be remade. The real estate promoters have already moved in: "Reichstag Revival Means Spending Spree," says a property maga-zine whose English editor views Berlin as Europe's hottest market.

"I see a lot of cars with Munich plates these days. That means money," says Alexander Dückers, the director of prints and draw-ings at the Dahlem museum.

Dückers's museum will soon move to a new site where forty-four firms are working solely on the engineering problems the new museum complex will raise in the new Berlin. A date for the selection of the city's final plan has not been announced. When-ever it is, says the architect Julius Posener, it will be too soon.

One of Germany's most honored architectural historians and builders, Posener, eighty-seven, began his studies in the 1920s when the 1910 competition to redesign Berlin was fresh in peo-ple's minds. He has watched his city change, much of the time at a distance as an exile from Hitler who went to Paris and Palestine, joined the British army, taught in London and Kuala Lumpur, and returned to Berlin to teach in 1961.

"It is extremely sad and very dangerous, everyone feels every-thing should move very quickly," Posener said. "I can't say any-thing about that because we badly need housing, but decisions made in a hurry cannot be removed in a hurry."

One quick decision that outraged Posener and many other Berliners was the sale of a chunk of Postdamer Platz to Daimler-

Benz for, it is said, one-seventh of its value. "It's quite disgusting. The senator who thought it should be sold hasn't learned any- thing because now an equally important bit of land is being sold to a Japanese firm."

The problem, Posener says, is the rush to Architecture with a big A with no preliminary studies of population shifts and in- come. How the city should look is the last question, he says. "First is how can we get this thing going and make it one city again? How can we save the many quite good houses in the east- ern part of the city which are in a very sad state, how can we add green space to preserve that aspect of Berlin which is essentially *Berlinisch?*"

What is *Berlinisch* is the low-slug horizon, the sprawling size (341 square miles) and the city's greenness, especially in such unique garden areas as Zehlendorf, with its wide streets, un- fenced houses and sudden dirt paths and trees. Posener grew up near Zehlendorf ("we never went into Berlin") and lives there now in a house designed by his professor, Erich Blunck.

Suggesting a neighborhood tour, Posener offers his wife's bicy- cle, jumps onto his nifty French model ("it is the cat's whiskers") and rides along, pointing out a white cube by Gropius ("a beauti- ful house"), a 1911 small house by Mies van der Rohe with curv- ing bronze grilles in homage to Karl Friedrich Schinkel, neat blue- shuttered double houses ("for SS officers, as Nazi as they could be"), Bruno Taut's mid-1920s flats on Onkel-Tom Strasse and fi- nally a tiny yellow 1930 house by Heinrich Tessenow that makes Posener laugh with pleasure. "It is a place of sorcery," he said.

The tour is a delight and makes its point: that small unconsid- ered places are as important to a capital as government offices and a building for Daimler-Benz.

It also makes an equally important unspoken point about mem- ory. What, in designing a new capital, should be remembered, what should be discarded and replaced? When should memory be officialized as history—and whose version of history?—or trivialized into nostalgia like purported shards of the Berlin wall, Russian caps, model Trabants, NATO penknives: the detritus of the tragic Cold War?

Memory is often inconvenient, and Berlin, living through enforced isolation as an island with its "Teufelsberg" mountain made from wartime rubble while the rest of West Germany bounded into the economic miracle, is a constant reminder of a troubled past. "In Berlin you could always know that Germany lost the war," Alexander Dückers said. "A part of the resistance of West Germans to Berlin's becoming the capital again is that without Berlin you can easily forget German history."

"The Germans have some reason to be afraid of facing history but then again they have to face it," Posener said. "Instead of facing it and asking how it could all happen, they repress it."

The Nazi monuments are all gone except for the Olympic stadium and a concrete slab near Spandau on which the architect Albert Speer tested weight-bearing capacities for Germania, Hitler's renamed and rebuilt future Berlin.

A question is what to repress now. Should the Cold War street names of the East be changed and in that case shouldn't John Foster Dulles Allee in the West be changed as well (and, to be politically correct, Onkel-Tom Strasse in Zehlendorf)? Can the Reichstag simply be renamed the Bundestag? Should the huge striding statue of Lenin in the East be torn down (Posener and Dückers say no) and was it right to put back the old Prussian insignia on the Quadriga of the Brandenburg gate (Posener and Dückers say yes)?

The answers are not easy. "We can argue that we have to live with history, that to bury it is unhealthy," Dückers said. "To say that the Lenin statue should be kept is perhaps historically correct but it is hard on the people who live there to be reminded every day of those cruel times."

At least 150,000 apartments are needed and rents have risen so swiftly that a carpenter who was paying six hundred marks a month had to leave when his rent was suddenly raised to four thousand. Dückers worries a lot about the city becoming boutiquized, yet he cannot help feeling a certain elation.

"I was born in Aachen in 1939. I remember when the city was destroyed and the joy of seeing it rebuilt. Today when I see a crane, although I know they'll do some bad architecture I still feel glad."

No one can say how many people will move to the new Berlin, traditionally the most cosmopolitan and welcoming of cities. "Anyone can become a Berliner, but if you were not born in Munich you will never become a citizen of Munich," Dückers said.

The mahogany and the curly cornices and the heavy tablecloths of Wilhelminian Berlin are gone, the asbestos-filled postwar housing of the East must go. No one knows what the new Berlin will be like and whether it will still be *Berlinisch*. Natan Fedorowskij, a forty-year-old Russian refugee who in eleven years in Berlin has done well selling what he calls Stalinist Romantic paintings, thinks it may be time to move on.

"When I first came to Berlin I came to a wonderful international city. Now it's just Germany," he said.

August 19, 1991

"LOVE YA":
VOZNESENSKY AND HIS COLLAGES

PARIS—Time was when the works of the Russian poet Andrei Voznesensky had printings of 300,000 copies and 14,000 people would attend his readings. Voznesensky's new collection of poems and photographs of his collages is in a limited edition of 1,000 copies and his latest poetry reading, in Siberia, attracted 3,000 listeners. "For Siberia, 3,000 is good," he says.

It isn't that Voznesensky's reputation is diminished but that life, and the market, have changed. The new book is a luxury coffee-table volume—the first in Russia, he claims—and it sells for the equivalent of $230. "There's a lot of new money around," he says. And in the dismantled, decentralized former Soviet Union there are many, but smaller, audiences for poetry.

These days, like a Westerner, Voznesensky worries about his cash flow and feels guilty that even so he earns more than most.

And in Paris he bought a pocket tear gas dispenser in case Moscow muggers do not recognize their potential victim as a famous poet.

Poetry is still in the genes of Russians and always will be, Voznesensky says, but his country is too full of old words, too much of what he calls blah-blah-blah. He is proud of his well-printed new book and of the objects it depicts because he says it shows that Russians can produce craft as well as words. "It is more important than blah-blah-blah. A minimum of words and more craftsmen. There is too much speaking in vain—slogans and populism—and nobody works. Nobody."

In the 1970s, Voznesensky wrote a poem calling the young the periscopes of the buried dead. Now he regards history as a burden and in a recent poem urged people not to be immobilized by memory.

"I think in Russia everybody knows enough about the past. If you speak of it you will only be depressed. All my life I was shouting about Stalin, Stalin, Stalin. Now they want to hear something more."

In the future Voznesensky thinks Russians should focus not on words but on visual images. He would rather appear on television than give a reading and he dreams of making films. His new collages, which he prefers to call assemblages, are attempts to express poetry in visual terms: "vidioms," or visual anagrams he calls them.

They were shown last year in a SoHo gallery, are on view at the Espace Cardin in Paris and will, he hopes, travel next to Moscow's Pushkin Museum. Two of them have been bought by the American artist James Rosenquist, one is in the collection of Jacqueline Onassis, and a chunk of asphalt with tank tracks representing the failed putsch of 1991 belongs to the Pompidou center in Paris.

Voznesensky, fifty-nine, was an architectural student until his school burned down, which he took as a portent to follow Boris Pasternak's advice and turn full-time to poetry. Along with his contemporary and rival, Yevgeny Yevtushenko, he won fame as an anti-establishment rebel. He was publicly attacked in 1963 by Khrushchev (an event commemorated in an assemblage called "The Poet and the Czar") and made a reply that has been called "a classic in any anthology of nonconfession." His poetic style was richly, and prudently, punning and allusive, and he saw himself as a tightrope walker with no safety net.

In the 1960s and 1970s he made many trips to the West declaiming his poetry with a stunning platform style (he once shared the stage with Laurence Olivier and held his own). He was cosseted and praised, translated by Auden, befriended by Robert Lowell. He met Heidegger, made lithographs with Robert Rauschenberg and on his current trip to Paris dined with Jacques Derrida. "Deconstruction is just coming to Russia. They are always behind."

He has written rock music, rejoices in the patronage and clothes of Pierre Cardin and has become an expert networker who these days punctuates his sentences with "darling" and hangs up the telephone with a "Love Ya!" But he is above all a poet and as such says he could never leave his country permanently.

"A lot of intellectuals have left but I think a poet must stay. That is why I am on television more than ever before, so that they know I am among them. Maybe there will be a civil war and maybe not, but you have to be there. I am not against people going to the West but a poet has to be with the people. It is something more than poetry."

He supports Boris Yeltsin's reforms but avoids formal affiliations and says he turned down an offer to become a deputy. "I am political but not political," is how he puts it. Speaking out for freedom in the old days cost him his freedom, he says, because it cut into his creative time. The young do not face these pressures.

"I think the new generation will be great, they haven't produced much yet but they are free and they read everything. Once they have really educated themselves, they will produce. I was free but sometimes too educated."

His assemblages range in subject from Madonna to a work called *Poetry in Russia?*, with blood dripping in a plastic bucket from the stem of the question mark. "Now the blood is coming from poetry but I am afraid it may be coming from the people," he explains.

The fear of a bloody future is also shown in a traditional butcher's chart in which the cuts of meat are chunks of the former Soviet Union. A similar chart shows the fate of the Yugoslav republics. *Self-Portrait of the Poet in the Twentieth Century* consists of two hourglasses bearing Voznesensky's initials through which vowels and consonants fall like grains of sand.

"A lot of these works are about the fate of poets which are not terrific—killed by the government or suicides," he says. In a work dedicated to Osip Mandelstam, the huge "O" forms the dark hole of the Gulag. Mayakovski, who killed himself while holding the telephone ("like Marilyn Monroe," Voznesensky says) is represented by a telephone dial bearing the letters of his name with a bullet mark in one of the holes. His tribute to Sergey Yesenin depicts the rope with which he hanged himself entwined with the scarf that strangled Isadora Duncan, his wife.

Prokofiev, with the part of his name that spells "coffee" enlarged, is flanked by a coffee grinder with a Kremlin dome signifying the government grinding down the artist. Similarly, a watercolor portrait of the young Voznesensky has a vegetable grater appended to it. One purely literary anagram spells out the name Proust with the final *t* seen, as if through the magnifying glass, in the *o*. "Proust is analytical, he watches everything," Voznesensky explains.

When Voznesensky made a poster celebrating Pasternak, the printer refused to have his name included for fear of reprisals, although this was in 1990. Voznesensky finds many of his compatriots shiftlessly paranoid. As a metaphor he tells about being attacked by three dogs last summer while on a country walk.

"Maybe they were hungry but I love dogs and usually they love me. This time they came straight at me. It is a symbol of our life because it is an undirected anger."

Voznesensky was saved by three passersby who took their time because, as he self-mockingly tells it, he was too conscious of his position as a great poet to shout anything as simple as help. "They thought I was acting because I cried in my poetry reading voice, Please people give me a stick so that I can defend myself."

In Moscow no one wanted to take the story for what it was, claiming that Voznesensky had been attacked by the devil. He couldn't make them see that real dogs had bitten him, leaving thirty-two puncture wounds in his legs.

"I will be marked forever, but luckily not on my face," Voznesensky said. "That would be bad for TV."

December 21, 1992

BRASSAÏ, AMONG FRIENDS

PARIS—In more than fifty years as a photographer, Brassaï has been much honored and loved, although less in France than in Britain and the United States. The compliment he likes best came from a curator at New York's Museum of Modern Art: Brassaï's portraits, he said, look as if the subjects had taken them themselves.

He is the most appreciative and least manipulative of photographers. "In a portrait," he says, "the most important thing is the eyes. I like them to look at me, and usually they do. I like the feeling that it is natural, but when I go to someone's house I can't say, 'Just act as if I'm not here,' because I am. That would be a false natural." How he gets his true natural is his secret; perhaps it comes from the fact that what really interests him is his subject and not the use he will make of him.

Brassaï is eighty-three now and recovering from a stroke, enormously touching and appealing in his eagerness and delicacy. He has always been shy, an advantage with the great, and those who think they are, as well as with the humble who realize at once that there is no condescension involved. Despite his long friendship with Picasso, Brassaï never addressed him as *tu*. "I didn't dare," he said.

In the mid-1930s Brassaï began to travel over the world for the redoubtable Carmel Snow of *Harper's Bazaar*. But he is best known for his Paris pictures—Paris pimps, prostitutes and other nightworkers in *Paris de Nuit* (1932) and in *The Secret Life of Paris in the 30s* (1976), Paris writers, artists and anonymous drifters, Paris graffiti—everything that caught his eager and compassionate eye.

The literary figures he photographed tended to be self-conscious (male writers, says Brassaï, often puff out their chests just before the camera clicks). His greatest sympathy was for painters and sculptors, and a book of portraits called *The Artists of My Life* has just been published.

Brassaï also wrote the book's texts, which are simple and revealing. Picasso was the most important to him, then Matisse, he says. He liked Kokoschka very much, but not his paintings. Bonnard was the most touching: When Brassaï went to photograph him, the painter was so filled with grief at the death of his wife that he would not allow his face to be photographed. Brassaï photographed him from the rear, a slight, bowed figure working at once at four unstretched canvases that have simply been tacked to the wall.

Brassaï always notices how his subjects use their tools. Braque's studio is orderly and stolid. Dali holds his tiny palette as if it were a toy while Picasso often has no time for a palette, spreading a cloth on a table and squeezing paint onto it and the floor.

The artists confide in Brassaï and gossip to him; the texts illuminate the personalities and familiar artworks in simple, graphic terms. Brassaï leaves high-flown analysis to others.

Giacometti, already tormented, is further disturbed by the fact that people often mistake him for Jean Cocteau. The aged Maillol pats the plump bottoms of his statues and thriftily saws limbs off plaster casts and attaches them to other statues. Le Corbusier's wife is dismayed at having to leave her cosy Left Bank flat for one of her husband's machines for living. ("It's like a hospital, a dissecting room. I'll never get used to it."). Dali when young is quite beautiful, with shimmering, hysterical eyes; the sober Rouault gets great pleasure in changing apartments as often as possible. Picasso likes dust because when it is disturbed he can see who has been poking around his possessions.

Picasso, whom Brassaï met in 1932 soon after he took up photography, is, along with Matisse, the center of the book as he was of the art world. If Picasso burns like an unruly flame, Matisse looks stern and surgical but in conversation is warm and measured. Picasso's front door has the word *ici* scrawled in huge letters by the artist, Matisse's has a small card: "Matisse, ring twice."

Born Gyula Halasz in Hungary, Brassaï took his working name from his native town. His father was a professor of French literature. In 1904 Prof. Halasz spent a sabbatical year at the Collège de France and brought the family to Paris. Young Gyula played in the Luxembourg Gardens, saw Buffalo Bill at the Champ de Mars and stood outside the opera on a gala night to admire Alfonso XIII of Spain.

"When I came back I didn't find the Paris I had in my head from childhood," Brassaï says. After art studies in Berlin he moved to Montparnasse and worked as a photojournalist for Hungarian newspapers. "Then I became scared because I saw that all those photos had no value and I thought I should do what I liked and I was right.

"The hardest thing in life is to live by what you like to do. Most people don't."

He was a gifted artist (Picasso arranged a show of his drawings), sculptor and set designer. The only film he ever made, a short, won a prize at the Cannes Film Festival of 1956. He never touched a camera until he was thirty.

When he first saw Brassaï's drawings, Picasso told him he had a gold mine and that by concentrating on photography he was exploiting a salt mine instead.

"I think I was exploiting a gold mine. The other arts came from the past—photography is of the present. I once said in an interview that photography isn't an art and there was a terrible fuss. But to make photography into one of the fine arts is to rob it of its novelty. Photography was an intruder among the arts."

Perhaps in part because of his novelty, Brassaï was a great favorite of the surrealists, a fellowship that he didn't find especially sympathetic.

"André Breton saw something surrealist in my work that wasn't there. I thought reality was much more surreal than surrealism. The miracle in life isn't the outlandish and the monstrous—it isn't the two-headed calf but the ordinary calf normally made. How awful to admire nature only at the rare moments when she does her work badly."

Brassaï still makes his own prints—not only prints for books and exhibitions but also humble reproductions for the press. His apartment is overcrowded with archives; he can lay his hands on anything in seconds. "Brassaï is a Virgo, very orderly," says his wife.

The outside world is retreating further from his Montparnasse flat and memory is starting to replace physical effort. These days Brassaï thinks more about writing than about taking pictures. He says with his sweet smile, "I would like to take pictures but I am too old to run."

October 29, 1982

ROBERT DOISNEAU'S
"LITTLE SCRAPS OF TIME"

PARIS—For the photographer Robert Doisneau the still, sad music of humanity has the sound of a fairground calliope. He chronicles fugitive moments, anonymous passersby, the beating heart of the faceless suburb. His pictures are intimate, tender and often funny.

"I don't like melodrama, the declamatory, the grandiose. I don't like people who speak in texts," he says. "I like things to be light, light, light."

For Doisneau, slim and rapid and sure at seventy-six, pain may be a part of life; it is not a subject. "Maybe I want my universe to be a lot funnier than the real one," he says. "I am photographing little scraps of time. Gaiety is perhaps saying too much, but moments when the weight is not too great.

"You don't live through three quarters of a century without sorrow, pain, misgivings, but why inflict them on others? It is true that misery is very photogenic and one can do wonders with a deeply wrinkled face. The ruins of Hubert Robert had a great success, it's true, it's easy. But a tree in bud isn't bad either."

Doisneau was born in the Paris suburb of Gentilly and has lived since 1937 in another suburb, Montrouge. The other day neighbors saw him climbing into his window because he had lost his keys again and they like to tease him about it. They also drop by to ask him to sign *A l'Imparfait de l'objectif,* his new book of memoirs published by Belfond.

He began the book because his wife is incurably ill in a nearby clinic and he stays at home as much as he can, to be close and bring her lunch. "I started to tell myself stories so as not to be sad." The title comes from the poet Jacques Prévert, who told Doisneau, "You always conjugate the verb to photograph in the imperfect."

Doisneau picked up photography at an ad agency that specialized in pharmaceutical products. His only training was as a lithographer, a craft that in 1929 seemed hopelessly quaint. "Having a lithographer's certificate was about as useful as a licence for a carriage would be to a truck driver."

After the ad agency he was a photographer at the Renault car factory for five years until he was fired for punching the clock late once too often.

"I was dizzy with joy, and terrified," he says. He has tried to avoid industrial photography ever since although the photographer he most admires now is Sebastião Salgado, who takes extraordinary pictures of working conditions throughout the world. "He doesn't take refuge in technique and he doesn't use other people's misery to heighten emotion."

When Brassaï, another friend, broke ground with his book on the seamier side of Paris nightlife in the mid-1930s, Doisneau took heart and persisted with his pictures of life in the Paris suburbs. The esteemed populist writer Blaise Cendrars befriended him—"he really cared about outsiders," Doisneau says, "Cendrars wasn't the sort who rubbed his thumb over a visiting card to see if it was engraved"—and wrote the text for a collection of suburb studies, *La Banlieue de Paris,* in 1949. It had no success but today it is a collector's piece.

"My childhood was the childhood of *la banlieue grise,* the gray suburb," Doisneau says. "It was so ugly that people were much more tender, the uglier it was the tenderer they were, in a way." He sees himself as a street photographer, ever mobile. The moment someone says "don't move" the picture becomes bad. He chooses his moment, of course, but finds Henri Cartier-Bresson's "decisive moment" a bit picky. Cartier-Bresson is a good friend whose rotten temper tickles him.

"Henri works in a state of tension. I'm dumb enough that if someone comes up in the middle of a shoot and says I take pictures too and brings out a snap of his mother-in-law, I'll look and say not bad, what camera do you use when in fact I couldn't care less. I don't want to offend. I should say shove off, I'm in a trance, but I don't dare."

What Doisneau does, he says, is wait for a miracle. "You have to be crazy. People come up and say, are you waiting? Yes. What for? I don't know. And you wait anyway. And then suddenly luck appears in the form of a silhouette more or less in the center of the frame. And then at that moment something happens that seems to ruin the whole thing and you say what is that idiot doing in the background? And then later you see that these intrusions bring something you didn't seek or expect."

A photographer with the Rapho agency for fifty years, Doisneau did fashion pictures for *Vogue* for a while, following Baron de Meyer and Hoyhingen-Huene and other monocled names, as he calls them. He hated it. He also photographed a flea circus and Gilbert, the fire-eater of Montparnasse, who was engaged in deadly rivalry with the fire-eater of St.-Germain-des-Prés. It's fixed in advance, Gilbert told Doisneau, those St.-Germain-des-Prés types have an in with TV.

He is wonderful with kids, shop girls, concierges' dogs, businessmen holding onto their hats in a gust of wind on the rue Royale, the sculptor Tinguely enveloped in smoke from one of his machines, a cinema queue, Paris lovers. He doesn't know how many people have written to say that they, or their parents, are the couple embracing in front of the Hôtel de Ville, but he writes back and tells each one that he or she is right.

He has had one lawsuit, from a man (a professor, he turned out to be) whom he snapped ogling a girl in a café. The experience so upset Doisneau that for a while he photographed only statues in public parks rather than people.

He says that rather than the *Mona Lisa* he would photograph tourists practicing their Mona Lisa smiles. "In what other job," he writes, "could I have got into both a lion's cage in the Vincennes zoo and Picasso's studio?"

The subjects are still there. Before photographing the actress Sabine Azéma that morning, he had a call from the man who runs the marionette concession in the Champs-Elysées gardens and he sounded a likely subject. But the settings have changed: His suburbs, once brimming with cheeky vitality, are now filled with bleak housing projects with windows like the holes in perforated cards.

But bulldozers are part of the nature of things, he says. "Beauty must be ephemeral. Museum cities like Venice are like old cocottes—only fit to be seen in a soft light."

A photographer, always at the mercy of light, can have no certainties, he says. He became alarmed when photography was judged significant, disgusted when it became the subject of philosophical and linguistic discourse. When the heart isn't there, he says, the label appears. Pure technique is barren: "The magnified structure of a crystal is beautiful. Beautiful and boring."

He says the camera is like a fireman's helmet: It gives courage. The only theory he ever liked was a dictum by an early critic: There are two schools of photography, soft and sharp. The advice his grandmother used to give him might also serve: Blow your nose, you'll see better.

His photographs, he once wrote, are all self-portraits, done with compassion and a bit of mockery and the secret hope of setting the established order of things slightly askew. "All this is absolutely not serious," he wrote. "Thank God."

March 20, 1989

PHOTOGRAPHER DON MCCULLIN:
"THE DARK SIDE OF A LIFETIME"

Don McCullin makes no attempt to conceal the distressing aspect of some of his assignments. Some of the photographs in this exhibition may be disturbing, therefore, particularly for children.

—SIGN IN THE VICTORIA
AND ALBERT MUSEUM

LONDON—All the photographs are disturbing, and since people do not like to be disturbed, some reactions to Don McCullin's retrospective have been odd. A lady from the BBC lambasted him because his pictures of famine and war were shown next to an exhibition of court jewels; the *London Times,* in a snippet titled "Over-Exposed," called McCullin lugubrious and joked that if he were to photograph England's green and pleasant land it would look more like Goya than Constable. McCullin thinks the *Times* may be right.

Some call him the greatest living war photographer, not a description he would like because he loathes the war photographer label—"There's nothing easier than photographing war," he says, "they drop dead"—and because there is shame in having survived.

He feels better after being hit by shrapnel in Cambodia: "After seeing so much blood of other people, it was kind of a relief."

McCullin is rugged, with eyes that seem to reel from too many impacts: a haunted man although he no longer has nightmares. "I used to have them even in the day. In Kensington High Street I could re-enact the sounds and smells of war." People in pubs sometimes call him a mercenary and then McCullin, a gentle man, knocks them down.

He is full of working-class reticences—"I have no qualifications," he says several times and he worries about his wife's reaction were he to photograph nudes—and while he tends to blurt rather than converse, sometimes a phrase comes out as old-fashioned and well turned as a line from a hymn. "Is it not a good thing that I stand at dusk in my country looking at a dying sun rather than a dead body?" he suddenly asks. He is amazed that his hair has not turned white and that he is, in his own phrase, relatively sane. "Despite my pictures, I'm not walking on my knuckles."

The pictures in the exhibition, reproduced in a book called *Hearts of Darkness,* are harrowing evidence of all we would like to forget or avoid. Wars in Cyprus, Vietnam, Beirut, Northern Ireland; famine in Biafra and Bangladesh; the lonely, crazed and dispossessed at home in England. It's a battlefield, all right.

An early photograph is of a placid London loony holding two skulls: "The Death Man," who robbed graves in Highgate, had a collection of human hair in his living room and whom, when they were growing up in a north London slum, McCullin's brother found very funny. The brother is now in the Foreign Legion. Childhood was brutish and at fifteen McCullin was working on a Manchester-London train and thinking things had to be different.

"I was programmed for my career," he says. "If I'd had a very good English background I might have been too sophisticated, too weak. I grew up on the dark side of a lifetime. I've always had the feeling that someone had a grudge against me, but I've never treated other people badly."

Compassion and reticence make his work so stunning: "The most scrupulously honest photographer," one of the best Vietnam correspondents calls him. The impact is undiluted by irony, sensationalism or the aestheticism seen in the late pictures of one of his idols, W. Eugene Smith. "He made Minamata into a kind of icon. I hope my pictures stink a bit. I hate art.

"The terrible thing about my photos, the thing that worries me, is that some of the people in them are dead. If you wonder why I'm so uncomfortable it's because I'm alive, I'm here."

McCullin isn't sure where his prints should be seen—on the sides of buses or in subways, he suggests, not in museums or homes. "I won't sell my prints for people to hang on their smart living room walls. If ever I see one I'll tear it down. The people in my pictures deserve not to be commercialized in that way. I feel guilty that I get paid but I'd do it for nothing."

To have earned money and to have won fame from other people's sufferings would have destroyed him but for his certainty that, unlike most photographers ("I wouldn't let the sods in, they break everything"), he approached the dead and dying delicately and with respect. "I was like a butterfly in the homes of the dead, I never disturbed anyone. I like to think—this is not conceit— that I was the right person to do this work because I never took advantage." Sometimes his camera viewer afforded him no protection: photographing a dying albino boy in Biafra, he says, "I was looking everywhere but at that boy."

McCullin shot his first war in 1964 and hopes never to shoot another. At forty-five, he knows that his legs aren't up to it; nor is his spirit. "I want to taste something different. I've been traveling around today looking at the skies of Scotland and it's bloody marvelous. Wouldn't it be amazing to be a Turner instead of a Goya?"

He yearns for normality, he wants to be thought ordinary. "I love getting pissed in bars and listening to the piano player and wishing I were him. My hero is Woody Allen. I wish me and

Woody could walk hand in hand down Fifty-seventh Street giving marks to beautiful girls.

"No one likes living more than I do. I've had enormous privileges, I've sat at tables with kings and traveled with world leaders—it's like a gift and I don't have any qualifications. But I think I do have the qualification of being a human being. If I wasn't inhibited, if I didn't care, if I didn't get drunk, I wouldn't be anything."

McCullin wishes for sunlight but he knows, as he says, that he can turn day into night. When he told friends in New York that he would like to stay there and take pictures, they urgently discouraged him, evidently fearing bleak and horrific results. "New York is full of good humor, it isn't full of muggings and sorrow," McCullin says, not quite understanding why they told him not to come.

He feels he is running out of options and wonders, because he enjoys clean sheets and bought a Regency sofa, if he has developed a dangerous taste for luxury. "One might start looking at the top of the wine list instead of eating junk food," he says, worried. Corruption, oddly, seems his greatest fear, but he says this isn't odd at all.

"How come three people next to me get killed and not me? Just being alive, I fear that corrupts me," he says.

December 10, 1980

CHRISTO IN SEARCH
OF A PERFECT UMBRELLA

PARIS—Only one person can make an engineering feasibility study into a lark: Christo, the artist who wrapped the oldest bridge in Paris, the Pont Neuf, in fabric and cord, who hung a vast curtain across a Colorado valley and who ran a 24½ mile fence along Sonoma and Marin Counties in California.

Christo's current project is called The Umbrellas: Joint Project for Japan and the U.S.A., and it consists of erecting and then opening 3,000 umbrellas at once: 1,500 blue umbrellas in Ibaraki province 72 miles (115 kilometers) north of Tokyo and 1,500 yellow umbrellas 60 miles north of Los Angeles, around Interstate Highway 5.

"They will be placed sometimes in clusters and covering an entire field, or deployed in a line, or randomly spaced from each other," Christo stated in his original announcement. "They will occasionally tilt according to the slope on which they stand." Both sites are farmland, with mostly smallholders in Japan.

The event is scheduled for October 1990, and like all Christo's works will take many years in order briefly to exist (the umbrellas will be open for only three weeks). Sometimes, when Christo has an access of realism, he isn't sure it can all get done in time—in addition to permission from local, regional and national authorities in both countries, he must get the consent of 51 landowners in California and 750 in Japan—and at such times he says well maybe 1991 or even 1992, but it must be October because then the summer heat has left California a lovely blond color, and in Japan the monsoons and rice harvest have passed and the country is lush and green.

The engineering feasibility studies will begin on May 2 with rented wind machines that can howl up to 150 miles per hour at a secret site in Cheyenne, Wyoming. But to make the study, Christo needs prototypes. He and his wife, Jeanne-Claude, have come to Paris to meet with some people who just might make him an umbrella.

Chief among them is Fredy A. Legler, a Swiss textile manufacturer with close-cropped gray hair and a briskly confident air. His factory in Bergamo, in the Italian Alps, makes the denim worn by five out of six Europeans, he says, and he flew himself up from Zurich airport in his own Falcon jet. He has brought a team of elegant Italian-speaking aides to meet with Mr. and Mrs. Christo in the drab suburb of St. Ouen, at the Rero factory (its owners' first names are René and Robert) where tarpaulins are made.

It was Rero's engineer, René Vidoni, who designed the Pont Neuf wrap and he is eager to have a stab at umbrellas. After a rousing lunch at a plastic corner café, also attended by the Magnum photographer René Burri and a St. Tropez hostess known as Tante Colette, the Rero and Legler teams go back to the tarpaulin factory to hear Christo make his pitch.

Christo talks with the persistence and conviction of a Fuller Brush man. Convincing the recalcitrant is an essential part of the art process, whether it be telling a Japanese farmer that tractors and trucks can easily pass under the umbrellas, which will be six meters high, or discussing liability insurance and easements (a deceptive word that always means difficulties) with California politicians. He never speaks of problems, just situations, and rather than admit that a project is impossible he will say it was put aside, transformed or delayed.

The Christos are almost always on the road, hawking and convincing. They have come to the Rero factory straight from the airport carrying two tin suitcases full of books and leaflets that were 36 kilos overweight. The day before they were in Copenhagen for lectures and dinner with the queen, the day before that it was two lectures in Oslo. At the tarpaulin factory Christo stands before maps and plans that have been tacked to the wall. His wife, the daughter of a French general who has strategy in her genes, sits with the guests and interrupts.

"The Pont Neuf was about art and culture, the umbrellas are about space," Christo begins, giving the history of the project (it dates from 1969, when the countries involved were the Netherlands and Japan).

The umbrellas remind him of nomads' tents. "We are making a poetic colonization," he says. Then, after remarks on climate, topography and population density, he gets into specifics: the umbrellas will be octagonal, with an 8-meter diameter. The diameter of the poles is 20 centimeters, of the spokes 7.5 centimeters. Each umbrella will have a 2,000-kilogram (4,400-pound) concrete base, sliced like a loaf of Wonder Bread into interlocking 20-kilo slabs that can be hand-carried. A pulley will open and close each umbrella.

For economy and in order to disturb the farmers as little as possible, there will be no trucks or cranes: only 810 workers in ten-person teams led by a captain. The workers will also guard the umbrellas in eight-hour shifts, shake rain from their folds and give out tourist information.

The umbrellas alone will cost Christo $3 million. "If South Korea can build a car for $5,500, we can make a parasol for $1,000," he says. Taking into account that daylight saving time will be over in October, available work time means that planting each umbrella can only take 6½ minutes. Because they are temporary imports, the umbrellas will not be subject to Japanese customs duties.

"The logistics are at a military level," whispers Fredy Legler, impressed. He is drawing diagrams and his aides are making notes. Enthusiasm is building so that work becomes play. The game's end is to enhance the quotidian briefly, to give it another dimension, which may be as good a definition as any of art.

But why is Fredy A. Legler, Europe's biggest denim manufacturer, sitting in a tarpaulin factory with his notebook? Because, he says, if he can bring Christo's enthusiasm to his factory workers, the results for his company's future can only be good. "Christo creates enthusiasm, which is something we can't do."

Nippon Steel and other corporations are also making prototype umbrellas for the Cheyenne test, for which Christo will reimburse them a symbolic $4,000 each. Some companies are astonished to find themselves competing to do something for which they can take no credit or fee, but this is Christo's system. He raises money through sales of his drawings, graphics and postcards, which is why he is almost always on the road. The Pont Neuf cost him $4 million (he paid back his bank loan this past winter), the umbrellas will cost him twice that.

"One manufacturer wanted to cover all our costs. Don't think I didn't have tears in my eyes when I said no," Jeanne-Claude Christo says.

Christo starts explaining what he wants from the umbrella fabric: a transparency that will give a play of light. *"Giocco di luce,"* says one of the men from Bergamo and writes it down. Fredy suggests using a nasty-looking fabric called openweave. Christo says no. Fredy looks briefly abashed.

Even the question of how to dispose of fabric remnants has been thought out. Christo is willing to discuss his artistic philosophy and the relation of the umbrella folds to those of the Pont Neuf if it is absolutely necessary, but he tends to leave this to others. Mrs. Christo passes out a book printed for Japan that has photographs of Christo bowing to farmers in rice fields and a scholarly article that opens with the phrase "Christo is a very polysemous artist" and goes on to discuss his work in relation to Brecht and to Russian formalism. The article is a bit cloudy because its quotations from Schiller and Walter Benjamin and from E. Fink's *Oase des Glücks* and *Spiel als Welt-symbol* have been translated into English after first being taken from the German to the Japanese.

The umbrella should not be stretched too tight, Christo says— *"un sagging au milieu,"* he explains, and a tension at the edges. Will selvage be used? Fredy asks. No. There is much talk of seams, and further diagrams. Is it possible to put it all together for Cheyenne? No. Yes! Everyone goes outside to see how Legler's polyamide blue and yellow swatches look in the light.

The samples fly off in the wind and serious people with briefcases chase them. The grimy court becomes like a school yard at recess. If everyone could only roll up their chic Milanese sleeves and start planting umbrellas on the spot, they would.

Everyone embraces and the Christos get into a taxi with their overweight tin suitcases. Tomorrow they'll be in the Netherlands, then Frankfurt, then home to New York. Fredy already sees himself on the test site in Cheyenne. He will pilot his Falcon there, he confides, going via Nova Scotia, which is the best route.

April 4, 1988

PETER BROOK:
"ONE HAS TO DO EVERYTHING
AS LIGHTLY AS POSSIBLE"

PARIS—The end on March 23 of the Paris run of Peter Brook's latest production, *Qui Est Là*, is, he says, its beginning, not only because it starts an international tour but because the project will always evolve. Brook regards theater as a process, not an end, and what he is studying here, having previously asked what is a play and what is an audience, is what is a director.

"I think the whole mystery and the whole question of directing can be resolved in the relations between two questions, why and how," he said in his office in the Bouffes du Nord theater.

The two questions are examined in the curiously effective framework—a mosaic, Brook calls it—of a compact version of *Hamlet* (*Qui est là,* or "Who's there," is *Hamlet*'s first line), interspersed with comments by directors and commentators from the

Japanese No master Zeami (1363–1443) to Stanislavsky, Meyer-hold, Gordon Craig, Artaud and Brecht.

"The first question, why do a play, can at first sight call up very superficial answers: Because it is a classic, because I think it will be a hit, because it is my job. It doesn't go very far because one sees that the theater form is beyond this.

"And now we make a little leap to the people in our play. What Gordon Craig was doing so dramatically at the beginning of the century, what Artaud was doing in passion and fury later in the century, was seeing beyond this into a form which is a whole mirror of human existence, visible and invisible. The more you face the question of why, the more one is open to the vastness of the theater potential."

For both Artaud and Craig, the stumbling block was the how, the concrete question of craft. "The person who is touched by the transcendental nature of human experience, the why, forgets the how. On the other hand, anyone who is acclaimed as a good craftsman and a real professional carries the danger that through their craftsmanship, their professionalism, their routine, the great why shrinks to the proportions of the how."

If Stanislavksy, Meyerhold and Brecht speak for the how, all five men were deeply affected, like Brook himself, by Oriental theater, which is where Zeami comes in. "The recognition was that even if the five of them together make a mass of understanding that goes beyond any one of them, this is the mass of understanding of Europe. The work of our International Center from the time we started in 1970 is to say the theater isn't bound by the European tradition."

The surprising high point of *Qui Est Là,* which Brook assembled with Marie-Hélène Estienne, comes when the First Player's description of a melodrama all too familiar even in Hamlet's time is given in Japanese by Brook's finest actor, Yoshi Oida.

"Shakespeare's intention is very clear, which is to have something in a style that seems purely theatrical and which because of the conviction of the actor becomes deeply moving. With the English text I've never seen it possible to get past the fact that for the audience this is so old-fashioned and bombastic that it becomes a barrier to his intention. It seemed to me that with an actor working with all the capacity that Yoshi has, one is liberated from any reaction to the language itself, so that one doesn't even bother to ask oneself is this badly written, do I go along with his style, these questions are removed."

Brook's career began, so to speak, at the age of seven with a four-hour "Hamlet" ("by P. Brook and W. Shakespeare") for his parents in which he played every part. As a grown-up he says he has never sat through a *Hamlet* without big moments of boredom and restlessness, including his own 1955 version with Paul Scofield, "even though we played it at such speed that we went through the whole text in record time."

Using *Hamlet* as what he calls a backbone for his research, he has omitted Laertes among others and he ends before the final slaughter with Hamlet's "readiness is all" speech. "Awareness, self-awareness, acceptance, renunciation, everything is in that phrase." Combined with the Japanese words for death, birth and life spoken by Oida, the effect is of peace and reconciliation, which is what Brook thinks audiences need from theater today.

The shaman is also a showman, as when Brook gets a laugh from the problem of getting Polonius's dead body offstage. "One has to do everything as lightly as possible," Brook says. "My own contribution—people say you're hidden behind these other directors—is in the act of selection, the making of the anthology. One is there.

"One of the bases of the work we do is that everything in the theater is play, *jeu.* What gives the spectator total relationship with the work is if it is played, not just acted." His analogy is with a football game.

"You can act without rhythm, strong actors in a bad play can be quite striking and yet you are unsatisfied because there is no rhythm. But a football match without rhythm is unconceivable and yet the rhythm is not the rhythm of a conductor, it's the living rhythm of a ball in movement.

"Within playing, humor, lightness, seriousness all fall into place as the movement of a ball which is sometimes quick and sometimes slow and sometimes stops for a moment."

The goalposts? "That's the play," Brook says. "A play is a very exact set of rules. And yet the playing is a complete circulation around these rules."

There are no secrets, Brook likes to say. This does not mean there is no mystery, and in the mystery lies the art.

March 9, 1996

ROBERT MORLEY
HAS JUST HAD FUN

DUBLIN—"Once when I was touring with Sir Frank Benson I wondered 'Why is he speaking so beautifully today.' He was hanging upside down in a tree as Caliban and it was the only position, my darling, in which his teeth fit."

Robert Morley was holding forth to a rapt audience in the studio canteen between takes of John Huston's *Sinful Davey*.

Story after story spilled out without a breath in between: the time he shared a cabin with a hermaphrodite on the boat to Cork; theatrical landladies; his mother-in-law, Gladys Cooper; acting with Marie Tempest ("You rehearsed in dinner jackets—the grandeur and splendor of it all"); the meaning of such arcane theatrical phrases as Responsible Gentleman ("It meant you played a lawyer or a judge—he wasn't a villain or a butler, just in between") and Dress Well On And Off ("It really meant you were supposed to wear your own clothes on stage").

"No one asked what a play was about," Mr. Morley said, walking back to the set. "We only asked how much and when did we start. Oh, it was lovely, my darling. Nobody talked about getting better. They just had fun."

Back on the set, Mr. Morley continued his monologue, punctuating each sentence with a grave little gavotte. He was wearing a pup-tent-sized kilt as the duke of Argyll and had just finished a highland games scene.

"I won everything I went in for," he boasted. "But then you'd expect me to, wouldn't you."

Mr. Morley was recently in America, where he argued about Vietnam on TV with Bob Hope—"I said the only people who understand this war are the resident comedians"—and plugged his autobiography. "By the time I was finished sales had suffered a sharp decline.

"The danger in America is people listen to actors. In England it's much nicer for the actor not to be taken seriously. In America they take everyone seriously, even the Pope."

"You look very saucy, Robert," said a passing lady.

"Oh, you are sweet," beamed Mr. Morley, twirling.

Next season he will be on the London stage in Peter Ustinov's *Halfway Up the Tree*, which Sir John Gielgud will direct.

"All actors like directing. It's nice not to have to be there after the first night and still get paid.

"You used to have very gay film directors," Mr. Morley continued. "Then they put in chartered accountants who sit there exuding patience. They shoot in regular office hours and make regular front office pictures.

"Hitchcock, for example, is one of those people who will have no nonsense. If you have no nonsense in films, what have you left, my darling? It's the only thing that flourishes in that climate."

"Coming from a long line of actors," chipped in John Huston, sitting down between takes, "I can say there's nothing duller than a respectable actor. Actors should be rogues, mountebanks, strolling players. Have you ever heard actors talking seriously about their work? It's my idea of hell."

"He and I were brought up in a world where acting was never discussed," said Mr. Morley. "It was like bridge or one's digestion."

"And yet actors today are better than they ever have been," he added, "and that's the result of self-examination."

"Let's not let them know it," suggested Mr. Huston.

For so good a character actor, Mr. Morley has made an exceptionally high proportion of terrible films. He isn't choosy about his roles.

"In my position I don't think it would have much point. I've enjoyed my life as an actor but I don't have a high opinion of my craft because early on I discovered anyone can do it.

"Anyway, when actors are stretched to their ultimate ability, they crack," Mr. Morley said.

"Remember when I first met you? I wanted you to play Nero," said John Huston.

"I never played Nero and I never shall play Nero," said Mr. Morley.

"I shall play Nero's friend. The witty senator, whose role is negligible, whose emotions are not explored, and whose makeup is deplorable."

There was a moment of silence, then someone came round to photograph Mr. Morley. He rose and posed gorgeously. "'Shoot,'" he boomed, "'there is nothing left to kill.' Do you know who said that?" he inquired of the set at large.

No one answered. "Really, you are most extraordinary. It was Gloria Swanson," he announced, beaming again.

August 11, 1967

BEFORE "PARADISE" AND AFTER—
CARNÉ'S PRICKLY RECOLLECTIONS

PARIS—The great period of French films was 1936–45 according to Marcel Carné, the director whose finest works, not coincidentally, span those years: *Drôle de Drame, Hôtel du Nord, Quai des Brumes, Le Jour se Lève, Les Visiteurs du Soir* and a film that is on most people's ten-best lists, *Les Enfants du Paradis*.

The last major survivor of his generation, Carné is stocky, prickly and to his mind insufficiently appreciated in France although covered with honors, including the rosette of Commandeur of the Légion d'Honneur, and a newly released film of homage, *Marcel Carné, l'Homme à la Caméra*, directed by the veteran Christian-Jacque. The film celebrates Carné's fifty years of filmmaking and, while grateful, Carné thinks it might have been better if he had given the director a hand.

When he speaks of the old days, Carné is critical of his

colleagues except for the director Jacques Feyder (whose assistant he was and whose wife, Françoise Rosay, starred in Carné's first feature) and the now-forgotten Jean Grémillon (1902–59).

"Jean Renoir always spoke ill of me; I think he was jealous. Then there was René Clair, but I didn't get on well with him. His films have aged badly. Grémillon made films that I thought very fine but that the public didn't like."

A painstaking and expert craftsman, Carné—who is about eighty but will not reveal his age—says he got his taste for work from his father, a cabinetmaker in the Batignolles district of Paris. After a year studying his father's trade, young Marcel, dapper in spats and slicked-back hair, alighted briefly in the business world before talking himself into a vague assistantship with Feyder that soon developed into a valuable collaboration.

His first film was a twenty-two-minute short, cinema verité long before the phrase existed. Inspired by his love for impressionist painting and by the fact that he had only a small camera and no funds for indoor work, he followed Parisian workers on a Sunday outing to riverside *guinguettes* where they laughed and danced and ate and drank until time came, sadly, to take the train back to town. The film was called *Nogent, Eldorado du Dimanche,* and Carné cannot fathom why people who see it today are so touched. "I don't see anything extraordinary about it," he says.

Carné has often been at odds with the public, the press or producers, sometimes with all three at once. Understandably for a man who continued to make feature films until 1973, he does not like it thought that his career ended with *Les Enfants du Paradis* in 1945.

He feels that there was a distinct plot, a *cabale,* he calls it, to bring him down and that it was led by the nouvelle vague. "They were critics before they became directors and they systematically demolished everyone who came before them in order to take their place. They were little arrivistes, Truffaut and Godard, people who wanted to arrive and who destroyed others in order to do so.

Chabrol, too." The atmosphere was not lightened when, according to *Le Figaro,* Carné called the nouvelle vague "congenitally impotent." Carné says he never said such a thing.

When he began making films, Carné says, the French were for the most part making awful light romances with people in *le smoking* going to casinos. "Then I came along," he says, "with my fog and lampposts and streets glistening in the rain." The film he is talking about is the extraordinarily atmospheric *Quai des Brumes,* with Michèle Morgan and Jean Gabin (1938). From then on, Carné was tagged with a label: poetic realism.

"I don't like the term," Carné says in his grand living room in Saint-Germain-des-Prés. (He moved there a few years ago because his doctor told him the air in Auteuil, where he then lived, was not good for him.) "I prefer the term *fantastique sociale* which Pierre MacOrlan uses about some of his books."

Drôle de Drame put the phrase *"bizarre, bizarre"* into the language (in the film it was uttered by Louis Jouvet in an eating scene in which Jouvet and his rival actor, Michel Simon, were privately vying to nudge each other into insensibility by drinking real scotch). *Hôtel du Nord* gave a new resonance to the word *atmosphère,* as uttered by Arletty, the great actress who is Carné's favorite.

"I never use the word *atmosphère,*" Arletty writes in her memoirs, "for it belongs to the public."

The dingy original Hôtel du Nord still stands on the edge of the newly gentrified Canal Saint-Martin in Paris, but Carné did his filming in a studio. Studio filming is a subject that makes him defensive: He says he was violently criticized for building a fake Barbès-Rochechouart Métro station when the real one was right there. The real one was unsuitable, he says.

"I remember the days when one had to film in a studio, you couldn't even film in a hotel room, for example, the equipment was too heavy. If the *nouvelle vague* made the cinema more mobile, the merit belongs not to them but to the engineers who came out with lightweight equipment and more sensitive film. If they'd had the material I had to work with before the war and just after, they would never have been able to shoot in natural decors."

If they were studio-bound, Carné's films seemed much closer to real life than the more conventional prewar product. Technically he was in advance—*Le Jour se Lève* with Gabin and Arletty was the first French film to be told in flashback—and in his fatalism and his distrust of *le happy end* he was reflecting the mood of the time.

"One felt it was the end of something, it was a melancholy time. In 1936 there was the Front Populaire, which gave great hope, then the war in Spain which one knew quite well would be the start of the world war. To make happy films in those days—I think one has to let the climate of the time come through."

The day after the invasion of Poland, a semiofficial article in a French magazine came out headlined, "Attention, producers! Make films that are healthy and optimistic." Carné and Renoir, the article said, had better change their style and start making films full of "courage and happiness and light."

During the Occupation, Carné avoided making films for the Vichy-backed Continental film company. With his collaborator from the days of his first feature-length film, *Jenny* (1936), the writer Jacques Prévert, Carné decided that their next film should be set in the past to avoid government interference. They chose the Middle Ages of *Les Très Riches Heures* of the duc de Berri and built a château that, like the château in the illuminated manuscript, was white because it was brand new (a lot of people thought it should look old, as medieval châteaus do). Arletty starred, the extras included Simone Signoret and Alain Resnais and the film, *Les Visiteurs du Soir,* was again a story of ill-starred love. The Devil, played by Jules Berry, figures in the story and there are lines that could be seen as allusions to the Occupation, but Carné says there was no such intention.

"There are lines that might be taken as attacks on Vichy but I don't remember, quite sincerely, that we thought of any such thing at the time. You must remember that we were very humiliated, shamed. There was in each of us—without our being aware of it—a surge to recapture by the spirit what we had lost by arms."

The next film was *Les Enfants du Paradis,* shot in the Victorine Studios in Nice and in Paris. Again, as an escape from interference, Carné and Prévert set the film in the past—in the colorful early-nineteenth-century boulevard du Crime, the Parisian center of theater and lowlife swept away by Baron Haussmann to make room for the Place de la République. The stars were Arletty, Jean-Louis Barrault (in a moment of panic when he thought he might not get Barrault, Carné considered signing a new mime named Jacques Tati), Pierre Brasseur and a newcomer, Maria Casarès, with clandestine help from the composer Joseph Kosma and the designer Alexander Trauner, both Jews in hiding.

"For me the film was an act of friendship. I never imagined it would have that success, none of us did," Carné says. "I never thought people would talk about it forty years later. When I'm filming," he adds, "I'm not much aware of what's going on around me, I'm in sort of a trance." Arletty once said that anyone who filmed Carné while filming could make a fortune.

"I make a film rather as if I am taking up a religion. There is a special atmosphere, though it may sound pretentious, that I have never seen on another set. Of course I am talking about the days when the crew was really attached, fixed, to the director. Today they talk during shots. Not only could I have not made *Les Enfants du-Paradis* without the actors I had, but also I couldn't have done it without that crew."

Carné tried to slow up postproduction so that *Les Enfants du Paradis* would be France's first postwar film, but it came out just before war's end.

During the Occupation, the collaborationist critic Lucien Rebatet had written that while Carné was not Jewish, he was Jewish-influenced, which was nearly as bad, and that he should watch his step. But after the Occupation, Carné found himself accused of collaboration before an ad hoc tribunal because he had continued to film. "It's a period no one can understand who didn't live through it," he says. He was given a public rebuke and his name was posted on the studio door. Arletty, who had loved a German officer, was imprisoned. To post-synch *Les Enfants du Paradis,* Carné had to ask the police to send for her.

"She came to the studio with two gendarmes and everyone turned their backs on her, even Brasseur. I was very disappointed by Brasseur. She had terrific guts. She had to do her first scene with Brasseur, very lively and gay, and she did."

Arletty, Kosma, Trauner and above all Prévert were Carné's team. The decline in his work is usually traced to his break with Prévert after *Les Portes de la Nuit* in 1946. "Prévert got bad reviews, worse than mine, and he said he was fed up with writing scripts," Carné says. He, understandably, bridles at Prévert's being given too much importance, but Prévert's contribution is beyond doubt.

No one can speculate on what Carné and Prévert (who died in 1977) would have done had their partnership not ended. Some of their projects that fell through are, like most fallen projects and some realized ones, mind-boggling, such as a life of Diaghilev with Orson Welles.

The real stunner was an idea that came to them just after *Les Enfants du Paradis.* Prévert and Carné decided to make a film of *Mary Poppins.* Unfortunately, Carné says, they were unable to secure the rights.

September 13, 1985

A RENOIR AIR OF FAMILY

PARIS—Jean Renoir, the film director and son of the painter, is back in Paris after a long stay in California. What does he do when he sees all those bogus Renoirs that blossom in Beverly Hills?

"Nothing. I do nothing. I see so many that if I thought about it I would be sick," Mr. Renoir said. "Sometimes I say, I wouldn't have bought that. That's all."

In Paris, Mr. Renoir lives in a hidden, tree-lined street in the epicenter of Pigalle. A few feet away are the blackened remains of the wall that once separated the city of Paris from the hunting fields of Montmartre. Around the corner lived one of Auguste Renoir's most famous models, Jeanne Samary.

"We have always lived around here," Jean Renoir said. "I was born at the top of the hill near the Sacré Coeur, which didn't exist then, and Renoir met my mother on the rue St. Georges.

"I like it here, it's not too pretentious. Here in this district you live in a caste system. The nightclub people don't mix with the shopkeepers and the shopkeepers don't mix with the old bourgeois like Degas, who used to live nearby."

Mr. Renoir has the pinkness, the plumpness, the small nose, wide mouth and air of solid joyousness that give all Renoir models an air of family resemblance whether they are related or not. He was wearing a gray pullover, baggy slacks and a pair of spanking new white Indian moccasins from Sears, Roebuck.

He is a towering figure in French films, revered by younger filmmakers, especially Truffaut. "I love Truffaut," Mr. Renoir said. "Not because he is talented—many people have talent, there are boring talents—but he has a poet's eye."

Mr. Renoir's *La Grande Illusion* (1937) is repeatedly voted one of the best pictures ever made. Now that *La Règle du Jeu* (1939) has at last been re-released, some people think it even better. Mr. Renoir doesn't think there is much difference.

"Any author writes only one book in his life," he said. "We have not so many things to say.

"I am not a real actor [he played a leading role in *La Règle du Jeu*]; as a matter of fact I'm not a real director. I'm a storyteller. In the beginning I thought it would be easier to tell stories in films than in writing. I was wrong."

Mr. Renoir has spent most of the past five years in his modern California house, which is almost engulfed by a huge wall—"I have the French mania for walls," he said sadly. He has been writing.

He has been working on a screen adaptation of David Garnett's *Aspects of Love* and is finishing the script of a film that he hopes to make in France this summer with Simone Signoret, Robert Dhéry, Paul Meurisse and Oskar Werner.

"The writing of a script or anything is relatively slow," he said. "I never understand a thing until it's finished. I'm not good at treatments—my characters have to exist, *then* I understand them."

The film will be in five or six sketches and is called *C'est la*

Révolution. "One good day someone says, 'That's enough,' and that is the revolution. My revolution is made of five or six revolutions, some of them real, some of them teacup revolutions.

"There is one man who cannot stand an electric floor-waxing machine anymore—you know the love of some women for the floor. But the main thing is not the story but the pace. It will be quick. Films today are too slow, except for English films."

Gallimard has just brought out Mr. Renoir's first novel, *Les Carnets du Capitaine Georges.* He has also written the absorbing and touching *Renoir, My Father,* and anyone who reads it will see how much of Jean Renoir—his love of craft, his feeling for friendship, his distrust of the intellect, his dislike of perfection, his sharp social eye—comes from his father.

"I think about my father very often, more now because I am not so young and I understand him better," he said.

One of the striking features of *Renoir, My Father* is the painter's quick humor. "He had no pretension to be sharp and witty," Jean Renoir said. "He just was. His way of looking at the world was primarily to be amused and full of love."

May 13, 1966

FRANÇOIS TRUFFAUT—
LOVE AND CHILDREN

PARIS—One might have supposed that François Truffaut was born with a silver Movieola in his mouth, but in fact he didn't see his first film until he was seven. It was *Paradis Perdu*, with Micheline Presle, and the year was 1939: Truffaut still remembers that the audience was filled with men in uniform and their girlfriends, who wept at the scenes of World War I.

He saw his next two hundred or so films by playing hookey and sneaking into movie houses; the fear of being caught gave him knots in the stomach and added to his clandestine pleasure. In 1947 he founded the Cercle Cinémane (Cinemaniacs' Club). The first article he ever wrote was on the director Jean Renoir who, along with the critic André Bazin, became his master.

"Was I a good critic?" he asks in a collection of his reviews made for Simon & Schuster, but published first in France (*Les*

Films de Ma Vie, Flammarion, Paris, 1975). "I don't know, but I do know I was always on the side of those who were hooted at rather than the hooters."

He left school at fourteen and saw *Citizen Kane* that year, 1946, when it was shown in France for the first time. He came to read Shakespeare through his admiration for Orson Welles, and through the work of the film composer Bernard Hermann learned about music, especially Stravinsky.

The cinema was his university and his high school, and the films he made could as a result have been as dry and doctrinaire as a Ph.D. thesis. Instead, Truffaut is the most accessible and compassionate of filmmakers, perhaps because he chose his master so well. A line from Renoir's *La Règle du Jeu* could be his motto: "The terrible thing in this world is that everyone has his reasons."

Truffaut has divided directors into two groups: those who have the public in mind in planning their films and those who don't; those for whom film is a spectacle and those for whom it is a solitary adventure. In the second group he puts Bresson, Tati, Rossellini; in the first group he puts Hitchcock, Renoir, Hawks, Lubitsch and undoubtedly himself. In his memory of *Paradis Perdu* in 1939, after all, the audience reaction is as important as the film itself.

This is one reason why Truffaut finds he works badly with well-known stars. "The audience already has an image of those stars, while the way I use them is against their image. My people are weak, vulnerable, fragile." The one triumphant exception was Jeanne Moreau, already a star when she made Truffaut's *Jules et Jim*. That, says Truffaut, was a rare example of balance between the role and the actress.

His newest film, *L'Histoire d'Adèle H.,* is a great success in Paris, as it was at the New York Film Festival, and features a twenty-year-old near-unknown, Isabelle Adjani, who gives a performance of remarkable intensity and intelligence as Victor Hugo's love-obsessed daughter. Truffaut is now editing *Argent de*

Poche (Small Change), which features two hundred children from the center of France.

Small Change is a kind of relaxation after the concentrated drama of *Adèle H.* "It's tiring, but it's a different kind of fatigue," Truffaut says. The film has a plot and planned episodes but the lines were mostly improvised. "I've always wanted to work with a 2½-year-old," Truffaut says. "Ours has a whole episode to himself and he is *formidable.*"

Truffaut first thought of *Small Change* in 1959, but instead his first feature film was *Les 400 Coups*. No doubt someone is at this moment preparing a thesis on Truffaut and the Child, based on his many films on childhood and growing up. One of Truffaut's own remarks might help for a start: "Adults are too taken with their own positions in life to be sincere. The only thing I can talk with them about is film, while with children I can talk about anything."

Like the other nouvelle vague directors, Truffaut was greatly influenced in his first film by Rossellini, whose assistant he was for three years (during which time Rossellini produced not one inch of film). "I loved Hollywood and he was very anti-Hollywood. He helped clear my head and taught me to recognize fake as fake.

"Also, he taught me a sense of economy. He said, you don't need money for filmmaking, you need it for living. He likes to eat rather well, you see. His films cost nothing."

Adèle H. cost only $800,000: Truffaut's ambitions do not require a Hollywood-sized budget and he isn't much attracted by the thought of working there since he has only been offered period pieces, including a film on Zelda Fitzgerald. "If I'd been offered *Paper Moon* I would have been attracted," he says. "I liked the story of the con man and the kid."

After *La Nuit Américaine* Truffaut stopped filming for two years and devoted himself to a long-delayed project: to go to Los Angeles and learn English. "I took lessons and lessons." He still can't understand English and speaks very little, but at least he can finally read all the American-published books on film. His office library ranges from *The Cleopatra Papers* to William Wellman's *A Short Time for Insanity*. On the wall is the news headline "Candidate Kane Found in Love Nest with 'Singer,'" and on his desk a photo of Lubitsch smoking the sort of big stogie Truffaut himself likes.

He will spend the Christmas holidays in Los Angeles. "It has become a kind of refuge, life there is so organized and quiet," he says. "New Yorkers are always mad at Los Angeles, they find the people too nonchalant." While in Los Angeles, he visits Jean Renoir daily and he showed him *La Nuit Américaine*, which Renoir loved. Renoir hasn't yet seen *L'Histoire d'Adèle H.*

"He may find it too serious," Truffaut says.

It is indeed serious, grave even, but never solemn. Truffaut's usual intimacy and charm are transformed to provide added intensity and movement. It is a superb film that Truffaut has worked on since 1969 and that is based on fact. "The authenticity gives the film a bizarre logic, which is not the logic of a scenario," he says. What attracted him in the tale of Adèle's unreturned passion for a lieutenant in the Hussars was, he says, "to make a love story where the partner is of no importance. Also, I liked the idea of making a portrait of Victor Hugo without ever showing him."

Still an admirer of American films, Truffaut dislikes those that have given a cozy Pagnolesque view of the Mafia or that emphasize violence: "I don't understand the argument that showing violence turns people against it," he says. In 1969 he wrote that the difference between American and European films is that American films are films of situation while European films are films of character, a view he still holds to with modifications:

"Americans have such a sense of adaptation, they have changed so they have become more European while still remaining American. A film like *Serpico* was so well written for the character. It could have been a documentary for the information it gave, but it was also interesting for the actor to play. Americans are much better writers, we have no screenwriters in France. In France, if a director has trouble writing, the film suffers."

Truffaut is dubious about film schools ("the extraordinary be-lief in America that everything can be taught!") and is heartily against the nostalgia wave that is producing such aberrations as Rod Steiger as W.C. Fields ("scandalous!") and a remake of *King Kong.*

"There is a real danger of getting something very abnormal. If you do a film on the 1930s, it's not on how life was in the 1930s, but on how the cinema saw life in the 1930s. I don't think it will last, it's not logical." Like all Frenchmen Truffaut has an excessive faith in logic. "It's as if one had erased the real history of America and only left the history of the cinema.

"I'm glad I did *La Nuit Américaine* when I did. I knew the time was coming when we would be seeing a lot of cameras in movies."

Truffaut has no definite plans after the release of *Small Change.*

"There will probably be other films about love and other films about children," he says. "Because that's the way they seem to split up."

December 8, 1975

ALAIN RESNAIS:
THE RHYTHM OF THE EAR AND EYE

PARIS—Just twenty-five years ago, Alain Resnais made his first feature film, *Hiroshima Mon Amour,* a film so startlingly original, Jean-Luc Godard said, that it could not be foreseen from anything we already knew about cinema.

Hiroshima came about in part because a producer had frozen yen to spend. Resnais had been hoping for years to make a spectacular adventure film, intergalactic perhaps (he is a great fan of sci-fi and comic strips), or based on Conan, the barbarian later played by Arnold Schwarzenegger.

"But the producers said it would have to be very cheap because only kids and a few oddball students would go. I said no, we must be grandiose and magnificent." So, had the producers' vision been longer and their purses deeper, we might have had a *Star Wars* or *E.T.* by Alain Resnais.

"Absolutely, that's what's funny," Resnais said, laughing. "The producers thought I would be too intellectual or cerebral," he added. "Maybe they were right but I don't think so."

The films of Resnais are indeed intelligent and demanding, but they are not remote and he is pained to be labeled an intellectual working for a narrow elite. "For thirty years I've been criticized for not making films for mass audiences. My pictures are seen by from 500,000 to two million people. Is it bad to work for only 500,000 to two million people?"

Resnais is pale, reserved and somewhat incorporeal, an impression he mitigates by talking vivaciously about the bread-and-butter side of filmmaking, by declaring that films are not everything in life ("to devote half your time to them is quite enough") and by laughing a good deal. It would be foolish not to call him serious but equally foolish to see him as solemn. He is working right now on a film script with the novelist Milan Kundera and says they haven't got very far because they laugh too much.

Resnais has warned Kundera that a scenario is much harder to write than a novel, a view that Marguerite Duras and Alain Robbe-Grillet, who had not written screenplays before *Hiroshima Mon Amour* and *L'Année Dernière à Marienbad,* have confirmed.

"Kundera believes me, I think, when I say how difficult it is, but it's hard to tell because we laugh so much. We are like young cats at play."

Last year Resnais came up with a comedy, *La Vie Est un Roman* (*Life Is a Bed of Roses* in the United States), which got mediocre reviews and reactions as astonished as when, with *Ninotchka,* advertisements proclaimed, "Garbo Laughs." His latest film, which was shown at the Venice Festival and recently opened in Paris, is *L'Amour à Mort,* an immensely moving love story, sustained at an almost unbearable emotional level, which deals with subjects people like to avoid—death, eternal love and the great beyond. "One must check one's Cartesianism at the cloakroom," one Paris critic said. Not everyone did.

It is a four-character film set in Uzès, in southern France. Two married Protestant pastors (André Dussolier, stolid and immersed in dogma, and Fanny Ardant, exalted and generous in her faith) are the friends of Simon, an archaeologist (Pierre Arditi) and his new girlfriend (Sabine Azéma). At the film's start, Simon is dramatically taken ill and pronounced dead, but suddenly revives (a recognized phenomenon with certain aneurysms, Resnais says).

Simon and Elisabeth, after this experience, decide to live life to the fullest but Simon, while never wanting to leave Elisabeth, is more and more drawn to the strange world he met in death (again, says Resnais, an observed reaction among those who have been pronounced dead and have revived). Then Simon has another attack and is really dead. Elisabeth, despite the arguments of her pastor friends, decides to follow him. "Can't you see," she says, "that I want to die not from despair but from hope? I am mad with hope." It is one of the film's paradoxes that love, not religion, gives a belief in immortality.

The word "death" in a title is a box-office killer. Resnais prefers to see the theme of *L'Amour à Mort* as separation.

"The most important thing in life is to find and to stay forever with our beloved. Death is obviously the most extreme form of separation but it isn't so much death that seems important to me in the film as the notion of finding, and then losing, each other— the suffering that comes from being cut off from your beloved, the need one has to touch, the feeling that your arms were made just to hold the woman you love. To lose that is unbearable.

"The film is built around that and also on the idea that you can die from love even if you are not Tristan and Isolde. It can happen to anyone. Elisabeth starts out as someone very ordinary and little by little she is illuminated by her stubborn hope. They are not extraordinary people at the beginning, not at all."

Resnais, sixty-two, was born in Vannes, in Brittany, of deeply Catholic parents. He was an asthmatic child (Simon's gasping in the film is all too familiar to him) and an early agnostic. "My parents told me I should be grateful for my illness and should offer my suffering to Christ because I would win a better place in paradise. It didn't work. I didn't have the faith. I was very obedient, but I didn't have the faith."

The four actors in *L'Amour à Mort* play together like a string quartet. "The actors were chosen in part for the timbre of their voices, for the combination of voices that I wanted. I am not a musician but I am very interested in sound." Sound is so important to him that he will even change a character's name if he doesn't like its ring when spoken aloud.

In *L'Amour à Mort* the quartet of actors becomes a quintet because of the score by the composer Hans Werner Henze, which is used as part of the plot to express Simon's changing moods and to incarnate the world beyond. The score is so important that the film could be called a musical.

"Yes, absolutely," Resnais says, "and the scenario is a libretto. The libretto was stripped of words, adjectives, poetic phrases and the music continues or replaces the words rather than just backing it up. Henze and I had long talks about the score and he knew that each time the music came in it would communicate something specific and not just disappear behind the noise of a car or the wind or the rain or the words. Since the score wasn't written when we shot, the actors listened to other Henze works on their Walkmen."

The music, says Resnais, comes in at nearly sixty different occasions. "It's absolute folly," he says happily. Many viewers did not share his joy over the score, dismissing it as cacophonic and, worse, contemporary.

"In the history of music, first performances are often catastrophes and obviously that is very dangerous because a film is made to be seen once, not twice. People have said to me, now if you had used Schubert or Beethoven it would have been beautiful. But they wrote for the concert hall. To use snatches of their work would have been improper, unfair even."

The libretto, or scenario, is by Jean Gruault, who wrote the last three Resnais films as well as scenarios for Rivette, Truffaut, Rossellini and Godard. Resnais has said that watching the screenplay be written is the hardest part of making a film (no, says one of his screenwriters, the hardest part is to watch Resnais watch you writing it). He has never used an adaptation from a novel and the screenplay begins with Resnais giving the writer a miscellany of ideas, images, characters, insights. "There is material one has in one's head and that comes out one doesn't quite know how," Resnais says.

Resnais and his writer always prepare a complete biography of each character. The late David Mercer, who wrote *Providence,* said that when Resnais first asked him to provide biographies, his reaction was, "My God, I don't know anything about these people."

"The biographies stimulate the writer and the actors," Resnais says. "If an actor asks me about motivation I can say, don't forget that he had this illness or that her favorite books are. . . . It creates a tie between actor and director, it allows more precise conversations and it makes the conversations warmer and more agreeable."

If a character is well drawn, he or she can surprise the creators. In interviews after the opening of *Hiroshima Mon Amour,* it became clear that Resnais and his scenarist, Marguerite Duras, disagreed about the fate of one character. Resnais resolved the conflict by declaring gracefully that a character is only authentic when he does something his creators don't approve of.

"I have always felt that," he says. "When people criticize me for having an actor do or say something, I say I am not making a documentary and saying 'I.' It is the character who talks, not I. And I try to give him the most freedom. With all the screenwriters I've worked with, I've always found that when the character gets away from you is when it starts to get interesting."

L'Amour à Mort is a controversial and, to some, upsetting film. But it is exemplary filmmaking in its phrasing, its movement, its apparent simplicity. Although it seems very still, the camera movements were numerous and complicated. "The camera really dances, but I think one has the feeling it doesn't budge," Resnais says. "The complexity is prodigious but, I hope, unnoticeable."

The rhythm of the ear is important to Resnais and so is that of the eye: he began as a film editor. "I think in terms of editing, I even think of editing when the scenario is being written," he says.

He began by making documentaries on subjects from alcoholism to the Bibliothèque Nationale. In 1955 he made *Nuit et Brouillard,* on the Nazi death camps, a task that must have left deep traces.

"It's hard to talk about the traces it left on me when I think of the traces it left on the people who lived through it," he says. "No, what strikes me most is that a film like that should shake people up—to see it so easily absorbed is a bit strange. One mustn't hope to shake up people with a film, but that doesn't mean one shouldn't try."

Married to Florence Malraux, the daughter of André Malraux, who has been his assistant since *Muriel* (1963), Resnais has always been respected but has not had an easy career. For a time in the early 1970s he made ends meet by lecturing at American universities. "The main difference between questions from French and American students is that the French were immediately moral—Why did you make this film? What use is it? Should money be spent that way? Americans say, you achieved this result, how did you do it? How did you choose your actors? They asked about the result, not the usefulness of the result."

For Resnais, the happiest moment of filming is working with the actors. "I lost six kilos during the writing of *L'Amour à Mort,*" he says. He is very lean. "And I put them back on when we were shooting." Unlike many directors, he loves actors and even listens to them.

"It sounds a bit boy-scoutish, but for me listening to them is a very important step of making the film. It's not a question of working as a collective but of stimulating each other.

"I remember my feeling of relief when I could finally work with actors—to look in the camera and see the face of Emmanuelle Riva or Eiji Okada rather than a machine tool or a factory floor!

"When I made shorts my consolation, my dessert, was to wait for the moment when an actor would come in and read the narration. I always got good actors—Claude Dauphin, Maria Casarès—and so at the end there was always that one small joy. To go from that, from having one actor for one day to having several of them for from four to six weeks—life has become so much more lively and gay."

September 28, 1984

IN RAUL RUIZ'S
CINEMATIC LABYRINTH

PARIS—Raul Ruiz is forty-four years old, a Chilean who lives in Paris and who since 1967—or perhaps it was 1960, it depends and who was counting and how—has made so many films that no one can reach a likely total, including Ruiz.

Last year he was in Portugal for lighting tests on his first relatively big-budget picture, *Treasure Island,* and while doing the tests he made three other films, as well as a three-part children's tale. Sitting in a room in the Los Angeles Holiday Inn and waiting to audition actors for *Treasure Island,* he wrote the scenario for another film. If sheer quantity suggests that his films are ill made or casually tossed off, this is not true. If it suggests that they are not always easy to follow, that much is certain.

His latest film, which opened to politely baffled reviews last month in four Paris movie houses, is called *L'Eveillé du Pont de*

l'Alma, and it contains several Ruiz themes—dreams and awak-
enings, personality switches, magic and death. The film's star,
Michael Lonsdale, said he certainly enjoyed working with Ruiz
but hadn't the slightest idea what it was all about since he was
given not a script but scraps of dialogue each day, which Ruiz
then either shot or not.

"He wrote scenes in order to get a story, which is the opposite
of the usual way," says Chantal Poupaud whose thirteen-year-old
son, Melvil, has played in five Ruiz films in a relationship reminiscent of that of Truffaut and Jean-Pierre Léaud.

Melvil plays Jack Hawkins in *Treasure Island.* So does Jean-
Pierre Léaud, who is now forty-one. The film includes an undis-
closed number of Jims and the pirates have become mercenaries.
It was shot in French and in English, which Ruiz does not speak,
and it was cofinanced by Cannon Films, the Israeli hucksters
now making a dash for artistic respectability.

Ruiz sometimes makes a film for $5,000 and he says having a
lot more money made no difference except that he had to use
American actors such as the TV veterans Martin Landau and Vic
Tayback, whom he came to like a great deal.

"American actors can be capricious though. They actually
want chairs to sit in between shots."

Ruiz is round-faced, amiable and married to another Chilean
filmmaker, Valeria Sarmiento. His conversation, like his films,
veers in unexpected ways ("The Assumption of the Virgin only became dogma in 1950. Eight years before Sputnik went up, she
did," he remarks over a plate of couscous, eyes rolled piously up-
wards), and his work is filled with untraceable allusions.

Widely unknown, he is deeply respected. Both *Cahiers de
Cinéma* and *Positif,* France's leading film magazines, have given
him special issues and he has had retrospectives in London, Rot-
terdam, Avignon and Madrid. His *Three Crowns of the Sailor* was
the talk of the 1984 New York Film Festival. "He is a wonderful
man, totally original," says Michel Ciment, a *Positif* editor. "He's

one of the few people who always avoid cliché and whose approach is somehow parallel to our own."

On the commercial side, he is pretty much of a flop. "None of my films do well," he says calmly. "There is a logic to them, but it drives people mad. I have a small public but it's always the same public, and half of them are professors of film." The first Ruiz film one sees makes no sense; after a few, one suspends disbelief. The other day, he held a marathon screening of the eight films he made in 1984. One of them was *Richard III.*

"It's pure Shakespeare," he said during the lunch break. "Except that I've given it a happy end."

The word *labyrinthine* is often used of his work but this suggests a linear approach, however cockeyed. Ruiz describes his world during lunch by outlining a rectangle on a tablecloth and quickly tracing diagonals and aborted little tracks within it. "He draws on all sorts of references, whatever he has in his head at the time," says Pierre Hodgson, who worked on the script of *Treasure Island* from Ruiz's outline.

Among the references in *Treasure Island* are Melville's *Benito Cerano,* an Iranian novel and G.K. Chesterton, whom Ruiz loves. In essence, Hodgson says, in an understandable cop-out, *Treasure Island* is a tribute to Robert Louis Stevenson. "You can see copies of the book lying around. The characters are playing a game around Stevenson."

In Chile, Ruiz studied law, cinema and theology. A supporter of Salvador Allende, he was also accused of rightist views when he criticized aspects of the Allende regime. After Allende's murder he fled to France, having received death threats, and his arrival in Paris was complicated by a Brazilian director friend who, when high on drugs, called the police to say that Ruiz was in fact the terrorist Carlos in disguise.

Like many Latin American artists, Ruiz is much influenced by British and American literature. "Faulkner and Henry James have the widest influence on Latin Americans. It is a way of escaping from Spanish culture, which is so narrow, so realistic—there is nothing more anti-magical."

The frame of reference he brings to his work is too wide to permit the tracing of allusions. A short documentary on the Loire château of Chambord included studies of Chambord as seen through the eyes of a medieval Thomist and the German philosopher Fichte. His inspirations range from Max Beerbohm's *Enoch Soames* to Margaret Mead. His technical virtuosity is stunning.

In Paris, he feels the pain of exile but also he warns of its dangers. Contrary to what Brecht said, exile inspires forgetfulness of one's native land rather than accentuating memory, he says.

"You become obsessed with small details in your new place— where to eat, how to find a flat. It can become almost a sort of fascism in that you think you are different, a special breed devoid of responsibility. It can lead to megalomania."

Ruiz's skill is officially recognized in France to the point where he was recently appointed codirector of the government-run Maison de la Culture of Le Havre. He intends to work there mostly on video, but will undoubtedly find time to make his own films as he did a few months ago when he was at the Maison de la Culture at Grenoble.

"It was fantastic, they had all the equipment there, all one could need, I had only to bring in the actors." He made three films during his short stay there—a rock movie, a sci-fi and his *Richard III* with *le happy end.*

October 25, 1985

WERTMULLER:
"I LOVE CHAOS"

ROME—From coast to American coast—although not perhaps in the three thousand miles between—Lina Wertmuller is the hottest foreign director around. In California she signed a four-picture deal with Warner Bros. In New York, there is much praise ("the most important film director since Bergman," says John Simon, usually a sourpuss) and the occasional clout ("despite the clamor of politics in Wertmuller's movies, her basic pitch is to popular prejudice," says Pauline Kael). At times it has seemed that every Manhattan movie marquee was flashing a Wertmuller title: *Seven Beauties, Love and Anarchy, The Seduction of Mimi, All Screwed Up, Swept Away by a Very Unusual Destiny in the Blue Sea of August* (which was abbreviated, thoughtfully, to *Swept Away*).

Now Wertmuller is filming *The End of the World in our Usual Bed in a Night Full of Rain* (which may finally be called *Night Full of Rain*). It is the first script she has written in English, and it stars Candice Bergen, who has rapidly learned Italian in order to survive, and Wertmuller's usual male star, Giancarlo Giannini, who learns his lines phonetically and is working like the very devil.

"Lina has given Giancarlo lines that would make an American actor tongue-tied—'Abandon yourself to the onanistic pleasure of the confession,'" Bergen quotes. She has been able to make her own lines more colloquial, especially Wertmuller's frequent references to the male organ: "Mr. Cock-break, the big sausage. We don't say that, Lina." "Ah," replies Lina Wertmuller with a sigh. "English is such a poor language."

A Roman of Swiss descent, Wertmuller is tiny, cocky, jaunty, filling the bucolic Palatino studios in old Rome with the demonic energy that informs her films. She wears white-rimmed glasses, rings on all her fingers except her thumbs and corduroy plus fours. She smokes a lot. "She's a little Napoleon. She's one of the most interesting people I've met," Bergen says. "She's like part-woman, part-man, part-goat, part-monkey, part-little girl, part-little boy. Mercurial. She's tougher than any man I've ever worked for. She's a tempest."

"Hard to work with? Me? No, I think it is very easy." Wertmuller says smoothly over luncheon meatballs in the commissary. She is itching to get back to the set and start screaming again, but she talks politely in convent-learned French from which, when she is expressing a complex idea, the central phrase evaporates into thin air. One suspects it would be the same in Italian. She prefers punchy aphorisms:

"I see the possibility for humor in the most serious things. Civilization is the possibility to laugh."

On making an Italian film in English: "There are lots of problems. It's like flying blind. But there is no loss of liberty. Liberty is an individual problem: If you lose it, it is your fault."

"In the act of writing or directing, what I like is *giocare*—to gamble, to play."

"I've done every kind of spectacle—marionettes, theater, films [she began as Fellini's assistant on $8\frac{1}{2}$]. An artist must do what he wants and he mustn't say whether it's good or bad. That's for the critics to say."

Wertmuller describes her films as Marxist comedies and her achievement may have been in bringing together these apparently contradictory terms. A Night Full of Rain is about a young couple. He is an Italian Communist journalist, she is an American sixties radical. They live in a flat so sumptuous (it was designed by Miss Wertmuller's husband, Enrico Job) that a rich aunt had to be written into the script. Against a background of modern tragedies from a San Francisco race riot to the environmental disaster at Seveso, the couple tries to live, love, fight, resign themselves. It is very funny and also very desolate.

"Lina does see that we are on the edge of a precipice, as do I after eight weeks of shooting. My nails are worn to the quick from hanging on. In the deluge—it rains all the time in the film—there is no hope for us," Bergen says.

Bergen, one of the few actors around with a strong sense of self-mockery, says now that they are shooting the scenes in which she breaks down, there is a certain difficulty in keeping script and life apart.

"Before, she was screaming, working in a fury. Now we're doing the intimate scenes, she looks stricken, almost quiet. The tension is there, but it's become very different. A gentle voice, 'Now Candina.' I am a fly in Wertmuller's web, and my own. I never used to be neurotic, now I'm neurotic and I see she's controlling it. I don't think I'm totally insane, but I've never experienced anything like this."

There is the language problem, with the director giving such instructions as "more strong your inferior lip" and "up your ass" (a defect of pronunciation, not an insult: the noun intended was your "eyes"). Above all, there is the fact that, contrary to Italian custom, the film is being made with direct sound rather than post-shooting dubbing, so the director cannot hurl instructions while the camera turns and must rehearse intensively instead.

"Since she can't talk during a scene, she compensates by orchestrating it," Bergen says. "Every gesture, every eye movement, is blocked to the millimeter." There is a certain irony here ("this film is a club sandwich of ironies") because Wertmuller told Bergen she wanted her for the first time to lose control of herself.

"She's right. I've never lost control in a film and I'm a little tired of being as controlled as I am. I wanted to divest myself of my armor, but this way of working, where everything is calculated, it's like working in an iron lung."

The precision leaves plenty of room for imagination. "She's very inventive," Bergen says. "She works off an immediate and very strong instinct and you see her building on scenes, adding a brush-stroke of anger, of neurosis. Her sense of detail is really mind-boggling. The first scene was a huge one in a piazza, with four cameras. She saw that my eyebrows weren't right. I said, Lina, aren't you upset by all this chaos? She said, No, I love chaos, I love anarchy, I thrive on it."

Wertmuller thinks this may be one reason she is appreciated in the United States and not in France. "America has a rapport with anarchy. America invented pop art. In France, art is sacred." She still feels it was bliss to be alive in 1968 and believes in the upheavals of that year but thinks life since has become much more complicated. "I do not see the road," she says. This may be why her present film is so full of obscuring, oppressive rain.

"Yes, I suppose the rain is symbolic," she says. "One says something is symbolic when one doesn't quite understand it. Everything is a mystery to the author."

And when does the author understand his/her film?

"Never," she says.

February 19, 1977

FATE, FELLINI AND CASANOVA

ROME—When a film is done it's done, and while it is being made it is in a process of constant change: Federico Fellini does not like to talk about his work.

"A film is made, not told about," he has said, and he fights with cunning against definition. Luckily, he is a skilled and fluent liar. Donald Sutherland, who plays the title role in Fellini's current film, *Casanova,* says the director once stated that *Amarcord* was the name of a Swedish doctor and gave an entire interview on that basis.

But fate has required Fellini to talk about *Casanova* for three years—when the project passed from one producer to another, when shooting finally started last summer for producer Alberto Grimaldi, when financially troubled Grimaldi cancelled *Casanova* in midfilming this winter blaming Fellini's extravagance, and when slander of the most ambitious sort flew around Rome (at one point Fellini was compared to Attila the Hun). Now, after more than two months of dispute, shooting has resumed with a reduced staff (cut from 200 to 125) and a shortened script. And so, once again, Fellini has to talk about the film.

"I've said so much, told so many lies over the past three years," he says, sighing a lot. When the time comes, he will talk in his office vividly and with charm—"He could sell railway stock, could Fred," says an English member of the production—but first he gives a personal tour of the set, the banquet hall of the dissolute duke of Württemberg.

Fellini is helping to dress the set for the duke's drunken revels with the care of a skilled hostess. There are sweetmeats from Sicily, oranges, dried fish surrounded by candied violets, conch shells that, he insists, say "Fellini, Fellini" when held to the ear, carved meerschaum pipes ("each one cost the producer $1 million because I am Attila," he says). He offers a sugar wafer ("that will go on the production bill") and says, "Now we will have a lunch, a little lunch like St. Francis." He makes a narrow gesture with his hands, "Because we are so poor." He is a most accomplished joker: The repetitious gibes about production costs suggest how hurt he has been.

"Fellini is a responsible man," says Donald Sutherland, who was outraged by the attacks. "He is not an ordinary director. He has to pull in resources that are not tameable. He lives on the edge of his fantasies, and that makes him vulnerable to the slings and arrows."

A motley crowd watches the shooting—chums old and new, a row of schoolchildren, a Casanova expert who cannot stay away although he disapproves of Fellini's view of his hero. On the fringes are the Cinecitta cats, as lamentably fecund as those of the Coliseum, and hucksters pushing fake Swiss watches and ancient paintings. Fellini occasionally uses a bullhorn and seems frantic.

"He has all these things in his head he has to get out," says Donald Sutherland. "He doesn't make you nervous, not like the little ones." Sutherland has been handed a long-promised six-page scene that Fellini had just delivered himself of and that Sutherland must learn at lunch. He doesn't mind. "It's an organic process with Fellini, like giving birth. The baby is born when it's time."

Later, in his office, Fellini says, "You have to invent a new life and give it more credibility than life itself, so that certainly has problems. Sometimes you feel sad and mortified, but all these things don't give you a feeling of sadness.

"To be a director gives you a sense of power, of fantasy, even if you have doubts. The possibility to create is in itself regenerating. I don't think God was unhappy when He was creating all the things He is said to have done.

"I am not talking about the result but the operation," Fellini says. "You are invaded by something else. I think I am lucky to be in movies. I don't consider it a profession, it is my life."

Italians may address Fellini respectfully as Maestro or Dottore, but he is also much criticized. He has never been forgiven by some for outgrowing neorealism, for being politically disengaged. Others feel he mocks his countrymen. *Casanova* may well be the most criticized of his films.

It is, he says, a film born of despair, disgust, a film of the void. Implicit in his statement is the suggestion that he is commenting on present-day Italy, for Casanova, to Fellini, is the typical Italian—an empty, attitudinizing, shop-front figure, an incipient fascist.

Fellini is shooting for the first time in English, thereby of necessity increasing his distance from his subject, and he is filming not in Casanova's native Venice, but in an extraordinary fantastic back-lot Venice—cold, foggy, unrecognizable, stillborn. The score has a lot of harpsichord; it also includes snatches from *The Rite of Spring* and from the funeral sequence of *The Clowns*.

Donald Sutherland, with hours of makeup each day ("Think of what *that* costs," says Fellini), looks remarkably like a contemporary pastel of Casanova—but redrawn by Fellini and stylized to the point where he is no longer flesh and blood, but merely line. He is always seen in profile.

Usually Fellini is enormously affectionate to his characters and it seems odd to hear him speak so coldly of Casanova. He is pleased by the word *affectionate*.

"People so often say I am cruel, that I make fun of people, that I am anti-feminist, anti-human, anti-producer. That," he adds of the last epithet, "is true.

"For the first time in a picture my achievement will be to show detachment, disgust, almost hate. There will be nothing human or familiar, no danger of identification.

"I could say that my great effort to reject Casanova, to reject Grimaldi, may be an unconscious fear to be like either one of them. That is a psychoanalytic interpretation I give free to the press."

Donald Sutherland, a very intelligent and supple actor, says Fellini chose him for Casanova because it had been suggested that he hire Robert Redford. "He said if I have to do it with anyone it would be Sutherland. They were so dismayed and he enjoyed their dismay."

A meticulous worker, Sutherland did considerable research on Casanova's life—and of course had to forget all he'd learned. "I said to Fellini in the beginning that I wanted to talk to him. He said we'll talk about it when it's over.

"There's nothing to do but jump when he says jump." Sutherland now jumps, gladly.

"He's a very funny man and with me he is like a lover—so delicate and fragile. He's a liar, secretive. Lina Wertmuller says he's like a man running along in a black hat and a black coat and he has this box in his hands and in it is a secret. Every once in a while he stops and seems to show it to you, then he goes on running.

"It's a wonderful world. You become terribly self-reliant after being used to working in a collaborative sense. This is not collaborative, it's participatory, so self-reliance is all you have."

Although he doesn't say so to Fellini, Sutherland became very fond of Casanova during his researches, seeing him as a hopelessly failed class jumper. "He was in such a panic to achieve it that he never really worked at it. He had no memory, that's why he had to write his memoirs. He was always in love because he forgot he had been in love before. You can be an optimist if you have no sense of the past."

That night after shooting, Fellini would be dining at Sutherland's rented villa on the Via Appia Antica. He never watches the rushes: Sutherland suggests this is because he wants to keep his fantasy intact, and probably he is right.

"If you see what you have done day by day," says Fellini, "you see what you have done, not what you want to do. You lose your drive, you need to go on in certain illusions you have in making your movie.

"What I have in mind at the start is only a fantasy. The real heart, the soul of the picture is what comes out later. At the end I don't remember what I had in mind at the beginning.

"You know why? Because I want to be free."

April 1, 1976

INGMAR BERGMAN:
A SHADOW OF THE FUTURE

MUNICH—Ingmar Bergman used to make his films in a small studio in Sweden with a small crew he called his "18 friends." The 18 friends loved him and protected him, and sometimes they joked about him because they loved him and because they hoped, unreasonably, that their mockery would show their independence from the unruly and incessant demands of genius.

Then, in January 1976, while rehearsing a play in Stockholm, Bergman was arrested for tax fraud. While he was at the police station his house and papers were searched.

His wife, a very wise and handsome woman, baked a cake so that the house would seem even warmer and safer when he returned five hours later, but this was not enough. Bergman collapsed and they left Sweden, keeping their island home on Faro, which Bergman does not consider Sweden. The only charge that has been heard against him was thrown out, but the wound has not healed.

"It almost killed me but if it didn't kill me it helped me, if you know what I mean," he said. The Bergmans went first to Paris, but within days there were two bomb explosions and a strike, so they came to Munich, which he describes as "a warm and open place to stay." He is filming *The Serpent's Egg* here, a big picture with a large budget and 350 extras, and Bergman's mood is expansive. He is coming out of his shell, people keep saying, which is reasonably true as long as one thinks not of a simple bivalve but of something like a chambered náutilus.

Bergman says that *The Serpent's Egg* is like no film he has ever made. Intensively researched, it is set in Berlin from November 3–11, 1923, dread-ridden days when a pack of cigarettes cost four billion marks. The title comes from a line in the script: "It's like a serpent's egg. Through the thin membranes you can clearly discern the already perfect reptile."

Abel Rosenberg (David Carradine), a Jewish circus performer, and his sister-in-law, a seedy cabaret singer (Liv Ullmann), are scrabbling to survive when they come across a terrifying clinic where one Professor Vergerus performs tests on human guinea pigs, all volunteers: "People will do anything for a little money and a square meal." At the nightmarish end, Abel has been shunted out of Germany and hears there has been a putsch in Munich. "The whole thing is a colossal fiasco," he is told. "Hitler and his gang underrated the strength of German democracy."

The company is working outdoors on a remarkable reconstruction of a Berlin street, cobblestoned, drab and meticulously detailed down to the 1923 Fascist newspapers that have been reprinted—not only the front page, which is all the audience will see, but the entire issue. The colors, says the cinematographer, Sven Nykvist, "are gray, as much black and white as possible. The best color is no color."

Knowing that his demands are likely to be enormous, Bergman works hard to create a state of enthusiasm and intimacy among his huge cast and crew. There are big smiles, loud laughs and constant touching—hugs, handshakes, shoulder taps. Everyone is happy. "He is a real genius, not one of those idiot geniuses," roars the ebullient German producer, Horst Wendlandt, who is so impressed by Bergman's economy that he gives him the highest praise a producer can give: "Bergman's not just a director, he's a *producer*-director."

The rapt devotion is easy to misunderstand: One can see why a British journalist visiting a Bergman set for the first time speaks of sycophantism, even if she is wrong.

"It is not quite true that I create the atmosphere, it is something we create together," Bergman says. "Everyone is important to the result. It sounds crazy, but that is the basic principle in organizing a picture. Then you must organize for the actors the feeling of security because if they are not secure they will be very unhappy and will make a lot of strange things."

Bergman's paternalism, his canny and effective way of getting everyone to give their best, extends to having Thursday night screenings of new films and to suggest on one day's call sheet that those who have not seen Fritz Lang's *Metropolis* should watch it on German TV that night. He sees the rushes only on Saturdays and says that, like Fellini, he could do without them entirely.

"I see them only because if I didn't I couldn't say to people it is good. It is for the people I work with—to be able to say to the prop man your newspaper looked very good, to say to David you were right, the first take was better than the second."

David Carradine wears an old cardigan that Bergman gave him under his jacket. "He wrote lots of scripts wearing this sweater and his wife sewed on the patches," he says with fierce pride. What drew him to the film was that "it's an Ingmar Bergman movie—a great individual type of movie, deep and somewhat not cynical, not pessimistic, but dark. Have you noticed in Ingmar Bergman movies that there is that tenderness? There is no villain, everyone is forgiven."

Bergman wrote the first draft of *The Serpent's Egg* long ago, in 1966, then dropped it. "I couldn't find the key." He describes it, only partly in joke, as his horror film. "Of course it is a horror picture, a real horrible horror."

One of the 18 friends in Stockholm once said, "Each picture reflects a period in Ingmar's life." The odd thing about this one, Bergman says, is that it reflects horrors, being dragged off to the police station, which had not yet occurred when he finished the script: "If you believe that the shadows of the future are seen in the present, then this picture is representative of that idea."

The script was an unconscious forecast of his arrest. "This picture is so different from anything I have made before and I don't understand why. I have no explanation of why this picture was written except as a shadow of the future. All January, I had the feeling, very certain and very strong, that nothing belonged to me anymore. I thought this table isn't real, this room does not belong to me."

When the vague feeling became fact, he was able to bear it. He plans to move his small production company to Munich, where his wife will continue to administer it. "She is my contact with reality," he says. His next film, *Autumn Sonata,* will be shot in Norway with Liv Ullmann and Ingrid Bergman. After that he hopes to film a long-cherished project, *The Merry Widow.*

Right now, and thanks, he says, largely to his wife, Ingmar Bergman seems to have a new serenity, although he is aware that any peace is relative. "In my profession," he says, "the terrible thing is that you are conscious all the time.

"An airplane has that thing, a black box. Even after the airplane has crashed, the black box is still going. My black box is always going," he said.

February 5, 1977

MARCEL OPHULS,
PROFESSIONAL MEMORY MAN

PARIS—Marcel Ophuls is a contradictory man, difficult, he says, and a bit paranoid. He worships the sunlit prewar films of Lubitsch and Capra and the films of his father, Max Ophuls, and he says accident made him become what he calls with uncomfortable irony "a professional conscience man."

Conscience means memory and Ophuls's documentaries— *The Sorrow and the Pity*, on occupied France; *A Sense of Loss*, on Northern Ireland; *The Memory of Justice*, on the Nuremberg war-crime trials; and now *Hotel Terminus: The Life and Times of Klaus Barbie*—are about memory, about bearing witness. Memory is the uncomfortable side of conscience: A "professional memory man" would be a better description of Ophuls, with none of the complacency that the word *conscience* can suggest.

Right now the strain is telling because he is in the last stages of editing the Barbie film with too much footage and a budget strained by the falling dollar. So right now there is Valium. The rest of the time there is a series of protective devices.

"One of them is to say that I am a hired gun, a mercenary of documentaries, which is true. I do it for a living and I didn't ask to do it, I started out on feature films." Talking about how the Barbie film began what seems like centuries ago with an invitation to write some articles about the World War II Butcher of Lyon for *The Nation* in New York, he interrupts himself: "You see I tell you this to prove that I go into these things by accident. I find it rather repellent that I would seem to be obsessed by these things, like a hamster turning round and round. I take the line in interviews that I'd rather be doing something else.

"What I feel really is that life is short and there are lots of other problems and *basta,* that's all." He knows it's by no means all, but one can hardly blame him for wishing to think so.

"And yes, the films should be amusing. One of the scandalous things that I should begin to say now is that on the good days, we have a lot of bad days, too, but on the good days in the editing room we laugh a lot. We laugh a lot because the picture is funny."

In *Hotel Terminus* Ophuls uses sarcasm as a way of approaching the subject of Klaus Barbie and his times. When he began his interviews for the film in Peru in 1985, no one was certain that Barbie would come to trial. Ophuls says the trial was to France's honor.

"I think it was important to have it because the alternative was not to have it. I don't believe in the educational necessity of the trial, not at all; you don't hold a trial like that for the young generation. And I don't believe in the symbolic value of the trial; I don't believe that individuals are symbols, whether they're mass murderers or not.

"I believe in the attempt to maintain mechanisms in a civilized society, to make differences between one act and another, to condemn one and acquit another. To make these differences—I think justice has to do with making differences. And, yes, with retribution."

Ophuls, sixty, feels he hasn't made enough films, and *Hotel Terminus* fills him with urgency on several levels. "It's a sort of comeback, it's a very big and very anxiety-ridden push to prove once more that it is me, that I can handle it and that I can do it again." There is another reason for the urgency: "I think the films and books on the subject now have to do with a feeling that if it's not done now it will be too late. It sounds awfully pompous, this business of keeping memory," he adds.

Maybe, Ophuls reasons, when he has shown that he can still do it, he will get a chance to stage an opera or make another feature film (his first, *Peau de Banane,* in 1965, starred Jean-Paul Belmondo and Jeanne Moreau). He has lectured on film comedy in the United States and has said that *Top Hat* is his favorite film. He would like to work again with actors.

"Actors are professionals, they get paid for what they do, they're specialists in what they do and they do it well. They tell good jokes. And I come from a theatrical family."

Max Ophuls took his family to Paris, to the apartment his son still lives in, in 1933. In France, he continued his career as a director of wry and elegant films until the dangerously late date of 1941.

"My father was a native of the Saar and so had become a naturalized French citizen. He knew the war would be lost, he had no illusions about it and there wasn't any kind of heroism, but he felt he should see it through defeat and not leave before."

The Ophuls family went to Hollywood and Marcel attended Hollywood High School. "I was extremely lonely, extremely vulnerable. Not part of the dating system. Not a football player. Sour grapes. A snob. They called me Frenchie, they called me frog." He remembers that his parents were rare among exiled Jews in grieving when German cities were destroyed.

Ophuls's wife is German and he holds French and American passports. He is at home nowhere and becomes furious with the

French when they describe his father as a German, rather than a French, director or add an umlaut to his name. In a sense he thinks the French will never forgive him for what he revealed in *The Sorrow and the Pity.*

"In this country people accepted the film because they had to, but you can accept the message and reject the messenger.

"Again, I think it has something to do with the accidental turn that this profession took. That particular film in this particular country. I guess I sometimes feel that I understand them and they don't understand me."

January 18, 1988

BERTRAND TAVERNIER
AND THE WAR THAT NEVER ENDED

PARIS—The nineteenth film of the French director Bertrand Tavernier, *Capitaine Conan,* is based on Roger Vercel's forgotten 1934 Goncourt prize–winning novel and is set in a corner of the eastern front in World War I, where the French, and British, battled the Bulgarians, Romanians and Bolsheviks. No one much knows about these battles these days, although the campaign lasted well after the official armistice on November 11, 1918.

The graves of five hundred French soldiers, all killed in 1919, are in Romania and the date given for World War I on the monument to the French dead in Bucharest is 1914–19. "On the Danube, about two thousand died nine months after the armistice," Tavernier said.

Given everyone's ignorance, Tavernier might have put an explanatory note before the battle scenes with which the film opens instead of leaving the viewer as baffled as the two Senegalese soldiers, their fezzed heads unprotected by helmets, who are briefly seen vainly awaiting orders from their French leaders. This is exactly what he did not want to do.

"I wanted no explanations during the film, I wanted the ignorance of the public—any public—to coincide with the ignorance of the soldiers about their own fate. I didn't want it to look as if the battles had been written and directed, I wanted to give the impression that nobody knows when it will stop, nobody knows where they are. It was a film that had to be shot not from the point of view of the general but the foot soldier."

The Captain Conan of the title, savagely played by Philippe Torreton, is a brave little mercer from Brittany whose acquired violence makes him into an outlaw. "For me he is a modern and interesting character. Can you immerse yourself in barbarism without being destroyed by it?" Tavernier's answer is no: at the end, Conan is back in Brittany, a drunken husk who cannot survive what he has done and knows, hopes, he will soon die.

"In the last line he says all the people who did as I did are like me, dead." Not all of them died physically, of course. Some may have become resistants in the Second World War though the more familiar example is Joseph Darnand, a World War I hero who created Vichy's dreaded Milice. "You have to die within yourself to do that," Tavernier said.

Within the film Tavernier is careful not to point the finger: Conan has a moment of redemption when he tries to defend an accused deserter; and his friend, Norbert (based on Vercel), has, amid all the confusion, to change from defender to prosecutor during court-martials simply to do the right thing. The one declared enemy is a familiar one—the vain and stupid generals who ran the war and who, Tavernier maintains, were even worse than Britain's generals.

"Two French generals were fired by Joffre because they fled in their cars when they saw approaching troops. They didn't realize they were English troops. There were not that many English soldiers shot by firing squad, there weren't the mutinies that are still kept secret. The English never had the red trousers which made the French such easy targets and which they had to keep wearing until the stock was used up."

French casualties in World War I were 71 percent, English 34 percent, German 63 percent, according to one historian. It is a subject Tavernier knows well, *Capitaine Conan* being the second of a projected World War I trilogy that began with *Life and Nothing But,* about the identification of dead troops with a view of choosing one to be The Unknown Soldier. (The bodies of colonial troops were not included, so one certain thing about The Unknown Soldier is that he is white.) In Tavernier's view the tomb was a way of burying the war and its memories.

Although, or perhaps because, it was such a cataclysm, the French have made few films about World War I, which Tavernier attributes to the fact that memory itself is a divisive factor here. He rightly points out that France is not alone in neglecting uncomfortable historical events: "Until the Ken Burns documentary how many American films simply lied about the Civil War?" If he ever made an American film he would like it to be about the noble and tragic Robert E. Lee.

Tavernier, fifty-five, thinks more about film than about his own trajectory as a successful filmmaker. He is the encyclopedic co-author of a dictionary of American film, edits a series of obscure film texts for Actes Sud and is the head of the Institut Lumière in Lyon. More than any director, he feels part of the history and memory of French cinema.

He has said he finds current French film anorexic and has deliberately tried to make his last three pictures as fast paced as Hollywood product, which is all French kids want to see. He spends a lot of time talking to schools in the bleaker suburbs and in housing projects.

"I feel it is part of my responsibility. It's tiring but I feel these people are deserted, especially the teachers, and I am getting a terrific response." The kids like *L'Appât,* his film about juvenile crime, and its police thriller predecessor, *L. 627.* They didn't warm much to *Conan.*

Tavernier has made easier films but feels that 1914–18 was the most important moment of this century, when four empires fell, the seeds of communism and fascism burgeoned, institutions such as the future UN and the Loterie Nationale were born and the world was remapped with consequences that we live today. "You discover all the time things that have their roots there," he said.

"That's one of the reasons I go to all those schools. A lot of the very young, when you talk about memory, are not interested. They all want to see *L. 627,* to get them to *Conan* is harder. But around Verdun you have miles of land which is made one-third of steel, one-third of human remains, one-third of soil. It is frightening for a country when its land remembers more than its people."

November 30, 1996

ELLA MAILLART
AT HER JOURNEY'S END

PARIS—At the age of ninety, Ella Maillart is no more ready to go gentle into that good night than she was ready in her prime to go gentle into that good day. Such is not the traveler's way and even as a young wanderer and sportswoman she was restless and, for a well-brought-up Swiss, unruly: obsessed, she has said, with the geographic reality of the earth, feeling the latitudes, each with its own color. Now, relative immobility makes her cantankerous.

"I would like to be in accord with this mad world and I'm grumbling all the time," she said.

She had just ticked off a radio journalist for asking boring questions (she later apologized). Her blue eyes are like bubbles of glass, her white hair is waved and tidily secured by a bobby pin, the colors she is wearing are bright. Her hearing is dull, her mind is not. She lived a life of action to get to know the globe and herself, and she thinks her knowledge is slight in view of man's un-ending folly. A doctor is useful, she says, and an engineer, but she is not. "I see problems, I have no solutions." It doesn't make for a peaceful old age.

Maillart, a doughty survivor of the last great age of travel between the two world wars, had come to Paris for an exhibition of her pho-tographs at the Swiss Cultural Center in the Marais. "How lucky we were—not merely at the time but in retrospect," Peter Fleming, her companion on her most famous trip, wrote to her in 1971. "Nobody will have the charm of doing, in whatever part of the world, that sort of thing again."

Fleming, Ian Fleming's younger brother, belonged to the Old Etonian school of travel writing—graceful and willfully amateur-ish. Maillart's books are plodding by comparison, in part because her view of travel is literally pedestrian, in part because she wrote only to finance her trips.

"I hate writing because it takes so much time. I am neither a good writer in French nor in English. My French is not com-pletely good because I thought and traveled in English, my En-glish is not perfect because I never learned it properly."

Taking pictures was marginally better, "It was quicker and less tiring than taking notes." Her photographs are a sharp and sometimes striking form of road map. She says that her aim in travel was self-knowledge and she likes to quote the line from Henri Michaux, "The shortest road to oneself goes around the world."

Her father was a furrier in Geneva, her Danish mother liked sports. Ella had a stubborn chin and, like many of the English travel writers of her generation, a profound disgust for the horrors of World War I.

"I wanted to leave Europe, go as far as possible," she said.

She bought a map of the South Pacific and, having already sailed the Mediterranean with a childhood friend, Miette de Saussure (later the mother of Delphine Seyrig, the actress), she

Ella Maillart in Turkestan, 1932

thought of heading to happy islands with an all-girl crew. Miette fell ill, and the trip was off.

Ella taught French in Wales, and became a secretary and a traveling saleswoman. She sailed and skied on the Swiss team and founded the first women's field hockey club in Switzerland. She was an actress, a sculptor's model and a stuntwoman in the UFA studio in Berlin while *The Blue Angel* was being shot there.

Helped by a fifty-dollar gift from Jack London, she went from Berlin to Moscow, where she met Pudovkin, walked across the Caucasus, tried to field a women's hockey team, and rowed for the Alimentation Workers Eight. In 1932 she went to Russian Turkestan. Introduced to a Paris publisher by the great yachtsman Alain Gerbault, whom she had met while sailing on the Riviera, she wrote two books.

In England, she had a somewhat glamorous reputation because the admiral of the fleet had received an official reprimand after the entire Mediterranean fleet missed lights-out while the admiral entertained Ella and three other young yachtswomen at dinner. Peter Fleming, a correspondent for the *Times,* had heard the story. Like Maillart he was eager to go to Sinkiang, in Chinese Turkestan, which was closed to foreigners. In 1935 they set off from Peking, reached their goal and then ended in Kashmir, 3,500 miles and seven months later.

Each preferred solo travel. Maillart decided it might be prudent to have Fleming along in case she were imprisoned; Fleming must have sensed that she was a lot more frugal and handy than he was, able to design and make a tent, cook outdoors in freezing winds, sew, walk fourteen hours without food and willing to wash his clothes. "It was she, and not I, who did the dirty work," Fleming wrote later in *News from Tartary.*

Maillart packed the minimum. Fleming took along Macaulay's *History of England,* a rook rifle, two pounds of marmalade, a bottle of Worcester sauce and writing paper headed The Times Foreign and Imperial Department. He called his horse Greys, she called hers Slalom. Both animals had to be abandoned when their strength failed.

Ella Maillart, Fleming wrote, was a gallant traveler and a good companion, and he suspected that the reason they got on was that she had a sneaking contempt for him and he had a sneaking respect for her: "Both sentiments arose from the fact that she was a professional and I was eternally the amateur. . . . We both knew that she was, so to speak, the better man."

Fleming, Maillart says, was charming and gifted and fundamentally unhappy. "We laughed at each other, I think that was the main thing."

At the end of the often frightful trip, Maillart wrote that she was sad: "It was the end of the easy life." It seems an extraordinary phrase but privations chosen are a kind of luxury, and concentrating each moment on survival is as good an escape as any from conventional demands.

Maillart continued to travel, although less spectacularly, and made her last big trip in 1986 when she led a group of tourists to Lhasa. Now she spends the summers in a mountain chalet and in the winters descends to Geneva, which depresses her. She may fly to Goa at Christmas.

She never had the illusion that she was an explorer or in any way an expert ("I knew the countries I had crossed only superficially"). She did not research her trips in advance.

"I never knew if I would have the permit. Why read in advance if I am not allowed in? I always aimed at countries that were difficult because I needed the sense of challenge. Nobody can go? Then I shall go!"

The only challenge left to her now, she says, is to die happy, with a smile. But a world filled with thriving arms merchants gives her little cause to smile. "How can I smile when I see our madness?"

She is incapable of the comforts of nostalgia, having always as a sailor and a skier and a voyager had to concentrate on the present moment. At her age, the present is inhibited and the future does not exist.

One of her favorite quotations is from Baudelaire: "The cat explores his habitat before he sleeps." She sees the earth, wasted as it is, as her habitat, and she is not ready to sleep.

November 6, 1993

A LOST WORLD IN PARIS

PARIS—A home that became a museum, a museum that hopes to resemble a home: the Musée Nissim de Camondo on the edge of the Parc Monceau is an intimate monument to the late eighteenth century seen through the lens of the late nineteenth. Its Louis XVI furnishings are a reference point to scholars and collectors; its atmosphere is reminiscent of cigar smoke and starched shirtfronts, Belle Epoque banquets on priceless Sèvres, carriages in the stables and children in the garden dressed in white. A safe world although there were already cracks in it.

The Camondo cousins, Isaac and Moïse, were very much a part of late-nineteenth-century Paris society, which had grown to include the banking world in which the family had for generations thrived. They joined such clubs as would accept them, entertained lavishly, collected fashionably (the Goncourt brothers had launched the eighteenth-century revival as well as participating discretely in another fashion, anti-Semitism) and found it unsurprising that the Paris *gratin* was willing to forget their origins in order to stag hunt or shoot at their country seats.

As a collector, Isaac de Camondo (1851–1911) ranged wider than his cousin, Moïse, becoming the talk of the town in 1881 when he spent record sums at the three-day Baron Double sales, collecting not only eighteenth-century furniture and paintings by Watteau and Fragonard, but also such moderns as Monet, Cézanne and more than thirty works by Degas. He gave his collection to the Louvre on his death, causing the museum to bend its rule about accepting artists' works unless they had been dead for ten years. Moïse de Camondo (1860–1935) concentrated on the late eighteenth century and it is his house that is the Nissim de Camondo museum today.

In recent months by coincidence two books have appeared on a family known more for its collections than its members: Pierre Assouline's *Le Dernier des Camondo* (Gallimard), popular history based mostly on secondary sources, and the more scholarly *Les Camondo* (Actes Sud) by Nora Seni and one of the museum's archivists, Sophie Le Tarnec.

In the few months since the books were published, attendance at the museum has doubled to six thousand a month, according to its chief curator, Marie-Noel de Gary, and a new catalogue is at the printers. Moïse expressed the wish that everything remain in place, a wish that has been followed insofar as this is possible when a private space becomes public.

It was in Constantinople that the Camondos first thrived in the eighteenth century, part of the Sephardic community that began to settle there after the expulsion from Spain in 1492. Despite the many restrictions and sumptuary laws that all minorities were subject to (Armenians had to wear deep purple, Greeks black, Jews blue), they moved from trade into banking, founding their own bank in 1802 and greatly enriching the Sublime Porte as well as themselves.

They gave generously to charity, even building a synagogue, since destroyed, in Lindos on the island of Rhodes, developed an entire section of Constantinople and, subject because of their religion to an innate sense of transience, had an alert eye for the pleasing as well as the profitable. They were known as the Rothschilds of the East.

Banned from Turkish citizenship, they became briefly Austrian and then Italian citizens and counts by fiat of Victor Emmanuel II while still living in Turkey. Paris, where they already had business connections and had spent several seasons, seemed a logical next step, and in 1869 the patriarch, Abraham, moved the family there despite his great age.

For Abraham the move was simply part of the family tradition of displacement and an opportunity to share in a vibrant financial scene. Social advancement was part of business success and adapting to circumstances was in his blood. Once in Paris, he quickly saw that Smyrna rugs would not do and ordered Persian carpets instead, as well as a large clock with allegorical figures representing prosperity. When he died in 1873 there was a funeral in Paris and a larger one in Constantinople, where all the city mourned, bells tolled, two battalions formed an honor guard and the bourse closed down for the day.

His son Isaac and nephew Moïse inherited property on the newly fashionable Plaine Monceau and a very different world. They made no attempt to become French citizens—centuries of wandering made notions of citizenship irrelevant—but they did become urgently Parisian. Softer than Abraham, they had no need to build a fortune but simply to manage and gently augment what they had.

They believed they could forget history and settle down. Unlike Abraham, they had no need to impress: they were accepted, within the familiar limits. When Edouard Drumont published his virulent *La France Juive,* they probably shrugged off such comments as, "One might smile to hear of the Count de Camondo or the Baron de Hirsch, but one becomes accustomed to it, almost."

Isaac described himself on his hunting permit as a landowner rather than a banker, which was classier and true. Although his father in his will had urged him to marry and carry on the family name, Isaac remained a jovial bachelor with an eye for dancing girls and neglected to legitimize his two sons, who died without issue.

His apartment on the Champs Elysées was a showplace, with art from Japanese prints to a Georges de La Tour. He adored music, helping to back the operas *Louise* and *Pelléas et Mélisande,* and his own composition, *The Clown,* was publicly performed with Geraldine Farrar in the leading role. Some critics compared it to Richard Strauss but the social leader Mme de Greffulhe wrote him that there could have been cuts in the second act.

Moïse, blind in one eye from a hunting accident, was less convivial by nature but as worldly as his position required. Balding and thirty-one years old, he made a marriage more reasonable than sensible to a beautiful eighteen-year-old heiress, Irène Cahen d'Anvers. She brought him a dowry of 1,050,000 francs, bore him a son, Nissim (which translates as miracle), and a daughter, Béatrice, and then ran off with Moïse's Italian horse trainer.

As convention required after their divorce, Moïse resigned from several of his clubs. He traveled, hunted, drove in a Paris-Berlin automobile race under his chauffeur's name and spent more and more time creating a fine new house at 63 rue de Monceau. Long an expert collector of Louis XV transitional and Louis XVI furniture and decorative arts, he commissioned the architect René Sergent to build a suitable frame for his collection. The model was the Petit Trianon.

Lieutenant Nissim de Camondo, 1892–1917
N. Matheus, Musée de Camondo

The project was to have state-of-the-art modern conveniences in a perfectly convincing eighteenth-century setting. It was a treasure house but also a home for Moïse and the children. The contents were, and are, stunning but—except for the tableware which Catherine the Great had made for Gregory Orloff—rarely showy. A small rolltop desk by Oeben is one of the outstanding beauties, as is the "Buffon" Sèvres porcelain, all the carpets and tapestries and the small "bonheur de Jour" table by Carlin with Sèvres plaques that took Moïse's scouts years to track down. For a treasure house it is curiously livable.

After three years of constant work, the house was finished. It was 1914 and young, affable Nissim signed up at once. He wrote loving letters to "Mon papa chéri," gave him news of society ladies' horses' performances under gunfire, asked for a cookbook since he had successfully improvised a macaroni au gratin for his men, and was given a camera by his father so that he could become a reconnaissance pilot. He died in combat in 1917 and Proust wrote Moïse a condolence letter in which he could not forbear mentioning his own poorish health.

In 1918 Béatrice married a member of the distinguished scholarly Reinach family and in 1923 moved with her children into her own house. Undone by grief at Nissim's death, Moïse continued to collect and resolved in 1924 to make his house into a museum in memory of his son. Moïse died in 1935 and the museum was inaugurated the following year, its furniture and Nissim's photographs left as they had been.

During World War II, Béatrice, fatally convinced that she was French, her brother having died for his country and her father and uncle having been among France's greatest benefactors, continued to ride in fashionable meets, a yellow star fixed to her well-cut jacket. The museum survived undamaged because it was state, rather than private Jewish, property.

"All those who really know eighteenth-century furniture come here," says the curator, Marie-Noel de Gary. "They are the true descendants." The only descendants, as a plaque indicates when one leaves this warm and wonderful house:

"Mme Leon Reinach, born Béatrice de Camondo, her children, Fanny and Bertrand, the last descendants of the founder, and M. Leon Reinach, deported by the Germans in 1943–44, died at Auschwitz."

January 31, 1998